# Chhatrapati Shivaji

## The Maratha Warrior and his Campaigns

# Chhatrapati Shivaji

## The Maratha Warrior and his Campaigns

By

Jeenet Sorokhaibam

# Vij Books India Pvt Ltd
## New Delhi (India)

Published   by

**Vij Books India Pvt Ltd**
(Publishers, Distributors & Importers)
2/19 (Second Floor), Ansari Road, Darya Ganj
New Delhi - 110002
Phones: 91-11-43596460, 91-11- 65449971
Fax: 91-11-47340674
web: www.vijbooks.com
e-mail   : vijbooks@rediffmail.com


Copyright © 2013, Author


ISBN: 978-93-82573-93-7

# Contents

| | | |
|---|---|---:|
| | *Preface* | *vii* |
| 1. | Timeline of Shivaji Maharaj | 1 |
| 2. | Introduction | 3 |
| 3. | Early Life of Shivaji | 67 |
| 4. | Shivaji and The Politics of History | 87 |
| 5. | Shivaji's Forts | 99 |
| 6. | Coronation of Shivaji Maharaj | 107 |
| 7. | Shivaji's Campaigns | 121 |
| 8. | Battle of Pratapgarh | 143 |
| 9. | Battle of Kolhapur | 155 |
| 10. | Battle of Pavan Khind | 159 |
| 11. | Battle of Umberkhind | 169 |
| 12. | Battle of Chakan | 173 |
| 13. | Battle of Surat | 181 |
| 14. | Battle of Sinhagad | 185 |
| 15. | Maratha War of Independence | 193 |
| 16. | Treaty of Purandar (1665) | 213 |
| 17. | Ashta Pradhan | 217 |
| 18. | His Legacy | 221 |
| | *References* | 231 |
| | *Index* | 237 |

# Preface

Shivaji was named so after Lord Shiva of the Hindu mythology as his mother was an ardent Hindu devotee. Since childhood, Shivaji was brave and never feared anything. He started a Crowning Era-'Rajyabhishek Shaka'. In the fight for independence and establishing his own kingdom, in every aspect Shivaji did everything possible.

"Shivaji is one of the greatest national saviours who emancipated our society and our Dharma when they were faced with the threat of total destruction. He was a peerless hero, a pious and God-fearing king and verily a manifestation of all the virtues of a born leader of men described in our ancient scriptures. He also embodied the deathless spirit of our land and stood as the light of hope for our future" once remarked by Swami Vivekananda.

Shivaji is known for his protective and fatherly attitude towards his citizens. He is remembered till date as a hero who worked for the welfare of his subjects and state. This book discusses his life and the campaigns he led for the country and his people.

— *Author*

# Chapter 1

# Timeline of Shivaji Maharaj

- *1630:* Shivaji born in the hill fort of Shivner.
- *1643-47:* Shivaji overran the hill forts of Kondana, Torana and Raigarh.
- *1647:* Shivaji's Guardian Dadaji Khondev died.
- *1656:* Shivaji conquered Javli from Chandra Rao More.
- *1657:* Shivaji came into conflict with the Moghuls for the first time by making raids into Ahmednagar.
- *1659:* Afzal Khan of Bijapur was killed by Shivaji.
- *1660:* Moghul Governor Shaista Khan occupied Pune
- *1663:* Shivaji made an attack on Shaistakhan's harem and wounded him.
- *1664:* Shivaji raided and looted Surat.
- *1665:* Jai Singh besieged the fort of Purandar and forced Shivaji to sign the treaty of Purandar.
- *1666:* Shivaji escaped from Agra.
- *1670:* Shivaji attacked Surat for the second time.

- *1674:* Shivaji crowned himself at Raighad and assumed the title of Maharaja Chhatrapati.

- *1676:* Shivaji's last campaign against Jijapuri Karnataka. Captured Jinji and Vellore.

- *1680:* Shivaji died.

❑❑❑

# Chapter 2

# Introduction

Shivaji Bhosale was a Maratha sovereign who founded the Maratha Empire, which, at its peak, covered much of the Indian subcontinent, encompassing a territory of over 2.8 million km². He was known with the royal title Chhatrapati Shivaji Maharaj. Shivaji as an aristocrat of the Bhosle clan led a resistance to free the Maratha people from the Sultanate of Bijapur and the Mughal Empire and established a *Hindavi Swarajya* ("self-rule of Hindu people"). He created an independent Maratha kingdom with Raigad as its capital. He was crowned as *Chhatrapati* ("sovereign") of the Maratha Empire in 1674.

## Maratha Empire

The Maratha Empire or the Maratha Confederacy was an Indian imperial power that existed from 1674 to 1818. At its peak, the empire covered much of South Asia, encompassing a territory of over 2.8 million km². The Marathas are credited for the re-establishment of Hindu rule in India. The empire was founded and consolidated by Chhatrapati Shivaji Bhosle. He created an independent Maratha kingdom with Raigad as its capital, and successfully fought against the Mughals to defend his kingdom.

The Maratha Empire waged war for 27 years with the Mughals from 1681 to 1707, which became the longest war in the history of India. The Marathas eventually emerged victorious. Shivaji pioneered "Shiva sutra" or *Ganimi Kava* (guerrilla tactics), which leveraged strategic factors like demographics, speed, surprise and focused attack to defeat his bigger and more powerful enemies. While Venkoji, the younger half-brother of Shivaji, founded the Thanjavur Maratha kingdom.

[Thanjavur Marathas were the rulers of Thanjavur principality of Tamil Nadu between the 17th to the 19th century C.E. Their native language was Marathi. Venkoji was the founder of the dynasty. Following the demise of Chola rule in the 13th century, the Thanjavur country came under the rule of the Pandyas who ruled for about a century. Following the invasion of Malik Kafur, the Tanjore country fell into disorder. The rule of the Delhi Sultanate lasted for half a century before Pandya chieftains reasserted their independence. Soon afterwards, however, they were conquered by the Vijayanagar Empire.

The supremacy of Vijayanagar was challenged by the Nayaks of Madurai who eventually conquered Thanjavur in 1646. The rule of the Thanjavur Nayaks lasted until 1673 when Chokkanatha Nayak the ruler of Madurai invaded Thanjavur and killed the ruler Vijayaraghava. Chokkanatha placed his brother Alagiri on the throne of Thanjavur, but within a year the latter threw off his allegiance, and Chokkanatha was forced to recognise the independence of Thanjavur. A son of Vijaya Raghava induced the Bijapur Sultan to help him get back the Thanjavur throne. In 1675, the Sultan of Bijapur sent a force commanded by the Maratha general Venkoji (alias Ekoji) to recapture the kingdom from the new invader.

Venkaji defeated Alagiri with ease, and occupied Thanjavur. He did not, however, place his protege on the throne as instructed by the Bijapur Sultan, but seized the kingdom and made himself king. Thus began the rule of the Marathas over Thanjavur. The Thanjavur Maratha Rajas favored Sanskrit and Telugu to such an extent that classical Tamil began to decline. Most of the plays were in Sanskrit.

Venkoji, the first ruler of the Bhonsle dynasty composed a 'Dvipada' Ramayana in Telugu. His son Shahuji was a great patron of learning and of literature. Most of the Thanjavur Maratha literature is from his period. Most of them were versions of the Ramayana or plays and short stories of a historical nature. Sanskrit and Telugu were the languages used in most of these plays while there were some Tamil 'koothu' as well. *Advaita Kirtana* is one of the prominent works from this period.

Later Thanjavur rulers like Serfoji II and Shivaji immersed themselves in learning and literary pursuits when they were dispossessed of their empire. Serfoji built the Saraswathi Mahal Library within the precincts of the palace to house his enormous book and manuscript collection. Apart from Indian languages, Serfoji II was proficient in

English, French, Dutch, Greek and Latin as well. The king was assisted in the administration of his country by a council of ministers. The supreme head of this council of ministers was a *Mantri* or *Dalavoy*. The *Dalavoy* was also the Commander-in-chief of the Army. Next in importance at the court was a *Pradhani* or *Dewan* also called *Dabir Pandit*.

The country was divided into subahs, seemais and maganams in the decreasing order of size and importance. The five subahs of the country were Pattukkottai, Mayavaram, Kumbakonam, Mannargudi and Tiruvadi. The ruler collected his taxes from the people through his *mirasdars* or *puttackdars*. They were collected right from the village level onwards and were based on the agricultural produce of the village. Rice was one of the primary crops in the region and the land used for cultivation was owned by big landlords. It was Anatharama Sashtry who proposed collecting taxes to improve conditions for the poor.

No foreign trade was carried out. The only foreign trade in the country was carried out by European traders who paid a particular amount of money as rent to the Raja. The currency system used was that of a *chakram* or *pon* (1 chakram = one and three-fourths of a British East India Company rupee). Other systems of coinage used were that of *pagoda* (1 pagoda = three and a half Company rupees), a big *panam* (one-sixth of a Company rupee) and a small 'panam *(one-thirteenth of a Company rupee).*]

Afterwards, Shahu, a grandson of Shivaji became ruler. During this period, he appointed Peshwas as the prime ministers of the Maratha Empire. After the death of Mughal Emperor Aurangzeb, the empire expanded greatly under the rule of the Peshwas. The empire at its peak stretched from Tamil Nadu in the south, to Peshawar (modern-day Pakistan) on the Afghanistan border in the north and led Expeditions to Bengal in the east. Ahmad Shah Abdali, amongst others, were unwilling to allow the Maratha's gains to go unchecked. In 1761, the Maratha army lost the Third Battle of Panipat which halted imperial expansion.

After 1761, young Madhavrao Peshwa reinstated the Maratha authority over North India, 10 years after the battle of Panipat. In a bid to effectively manage the large empire, semi-autonomy was given to strongest of the knights, which created a confederacy of Maratha states. They became known as Gaekwads of Baroda, the Holkars of Indore and Malwa, the Scindias of Gwalior and Ujjain, Bhonsales of Nagpur. In 1775, the British East India Company intervened in a succession struggle in Pune, which became the First Anglo-Maratha War. Marathas remained the preeminent power in India until their defeat in the Second and Third Anglo-Maratha Wars (1805–1818), which left Britain in control of most of India.

A large portion of the empire was coastline that had been secured by a potent navy under commanders such as Kanhoji Angre. He was very successful at keeping foreign naval ships, particularly of the Portuguese and British, at bay. Securing the coastal areas and building land-based fortifications were crucial aspects of the Maratha's defensive strategy and regional military history.

After a lifetime of guerrilla warfare with Adilshah of Bijapur and Mughal Emperor Aurangzeb, Shivaji founded an independent Hindu Maratha kingdom in 1674 with Raigad as its capital. Shivaji died in 1680, leaving behind a large, but vulnerable kingdom. The Mughals invaded, fighting an unsuccessful War of 27 years from 1681 to 1707. Shahu, a grandson of Shivaji, ruled as emperor until 1749. During his reign, Shahu appointed the first Peshwa as head of the government, under certain conditions. After the death of Shahu, the Peshwas became the *de facto* leaders of the Maratha Empire from 1749 to 1761, while Shivaji's successors continued as nominal rulers from their base in Satara.

Covering a large part of the subcontinent, the Maratha Empire kept the British forces at bay during the 18th century, until the Third Battle of Panipat following which Marathas never fought as a single unit. The Maratha Empire was at its height in the 18th century under Shahu and the Peshwa Baji Rao I. Losses at the Third Battle of Panipat in 1761 suspended further expansion of the empire in the North-west and reduced the power of the Peshwas. In 1761, after severe losses in the Panipat war, the Peshwas slowly started losing the control of the state. Many military chiefs of the Maratha Empire like Shinde, Holkar, Gaikwad, Pant Pratinidhi, Bhosale of Nagpur, Pandit of Bhor, Patwardhan, and Newalkarstarted to work towards their ambition of becoming kings in their respective regions. However, under Madhavrao Peshwa, Maratha authority in North India was restored, 10 years after the battle of Panipat.

After the death of Madhavrao, the empire gave way to a loose Confederacy, with political power resting in a 'pentarchy' of five mostly Maratha dynasties: the Peshwas of Pune; the Sindhias (originally "Shinde") of Malwa and Gwalior; the Holkars of Indore; the Bhonsles of Nagpur; and the Gaekwads of Baroda. A rivalry between the Sindhia and Holkar dominated the confederation's affairs into the early 19th century, as did the clashes with the British and the British East India Company in the three Anglo-Maratha Wars.

In the Third Anglo-Maratha War, the last Peshwa, Baji Rao II, was defeated by the British in 1818.

Most of the former Maratha Empire was absorbed by British India, although some of the Maratha states persisted as quasi-independent princely states until India became independent in 1947.

## The Royal Era (1674-1749)

*Chhatrapati Shivaji*

*Fig.: Shivaji, founder of the Maratha Empire*

Shivaji was a Maratha aristocrat of the Bhosle clan who founded the Maratha Empire. Shivaji led a resistance to free the Maratha people from the Sultanate of Bijapur, and re-establish Hindavi Swarajya ("self-rule of Hindu people"). He created an independent Maratha kingdom with Vedant Raigad as its capital, and successfully fought against the Mughals to defend his kingdom. He was crowned as Chhatrapati ("sovereign") of the Maratha Empire in 1674.

The Marathas had lived in the Desh region around Pune for a long time, in the western portion of the Deccan, where the plateau meets the eastern slopes of the Western Ghats. They had resisted incursions into the region by the Mughal rulers of northern India. Under their leader Shivaji Maharaj, the Marathas freed themselves from the Muslim Turkic sultans of Bijapur to the southeast under the leadership of Shivaji Maharaj, and became much more aggressive, frequently raiding Mughal territory and ransacking the Mughal port of Surat in 1664 and again in 1670.

In 1674 Shivaji proclaimed himself king, taking the title (Chhatrapati). By Shivaji Maharaja's death in 1680, the Marathas had expanded their territory to include many parts of central and south India. According to Indian historian Tryambak Shankar Shejwalkar, Shivaji was inspired by the great Vijayanagara Empire, a bulwark against the Muslim invasion of South India. The victories of the then king of Mysore, Kanthirava Narasaraja I against the Sultan of Bijapur also inspired Shivaji. According to the legend, Shivaji was the first king in India whose vision encompassed the dev (god), desh (country) and dharma (natural law, righteousness).

*Chhatrapati Sambhaji*

*Fig.: Chhatrapati Sambhaji Bhosle*

Chhatrapati Shivaji had two sons: Sambhaji and Rajaram. Sambhaji, the elder son, was very popular among the courtiers. He was a great warrior, great politician and poet. In 1681, Sambhaji had himself crowned and resumed his father's expansionist policies. Sambhaji had earlier defeated the Portuguese and Chikka Deva Raya of Mysore. To nullify any Rajput-Maratha alliance, as well as the Deccan Sultanates, the Mughal emperor Aurangzeb himself headed south in 1681.

With his entire imperial court, administration, and an army of about 500,000 troops he proceeded to conquer the entire Maratha Empire along with the sultanates of Bijapur and Golconda. During the eight years that followed, Sambhaji led the Marathas, never losing a battle or a fort to Aurangzeb. Aurangzeb had almost lost the campaign but for an event in early 1689.

Sambhaji called his commanders for a strategic meeting at Sangameshwar to decide on the final onslaught on the Mughal forces. In a meticulously planned operation, Ganoji Shirke and Aurangzeb's commander, Mukarrab Khan attacked Sangameshwar when Sambhaji was accompanied by a few men. Sambhaji was ambushed and captured by Mughal troops on 1 Feb, 1689. He and his advisor, Kavi Kalash were taken to Bahadurgad. Sambhaji and Kavi Kalash were tortured to death on March 11, 1689.

### Chhatrapati Rajaram and Maharani Tarabai

Rajaram, Chattrapati Sambhaji's brother, now assumed the throne. Mughals laid siege to Raigad. Rajaram fled to Vishalgad and then to Jinjifor safety. From there, the Marathas raided the Mughal territory and many forts were captured by Maratha commanders Santaji Ghorpade,Dhanaji Jadhav, Parshuram Pant Pratinidhi, Shankaraji Narayan Sacheev, and Melgiri Pandit. In 1697, Rajaram offered a truce but this was rejected by the emperor. Rajaram died in 1700 at Sinhagad. His widow, Tarabai, assumed control in the name of her son Ramaraja (Shivaji II). Then Tarabai heroically led the Marathas against the Mughals; by 1705, they had crossed the Narmada River and entered Malwa, then in Mughal possession.

Malwa was a decisive battle for the Maratha Empire. The Mughals lost their eminent position on the Indian subcontinent forever and the subsequent Mughal emperors became titular rulers.

The Marathas emerged victorious after a long drawn-out and fiercely fought battle. The soldiers and commanders who participated in this war achieved the real expansion of the Maratha Empire. The victory also set the foundations for the imperial conquests achieved later, under the Peshwas.

Ramchandra Pant Amatya Bawdekar was a court administrator who rose from the ranks of a local Kulkarni to the ranks of Ashtapradhan under guidance and support of Shivaji. When Chhatrapati Rajaram fled to Jinji in 1689 leaving Maratha Empire, he gave a "Hukumat Panha" (King Status) to Pant before leaving.

Ramchandra Pant managed the entire state under many challenges like influx of Mughals, betrayal from Vatandars (local satraps under the Maratha state) and social challenges like scarcity of food.

With the help of Pantpratinidhi, Sachiv, he kept the economic condition of Maratha Empire in an appropriate state. He wrote "Adnyapatra" in which he has explained different techniques of war, maintenance of forts and administration etc.

## *Chhatrapati Shahu*

*Fig.: The Mughal Emperor Muhammad Shah tried to halt Maratha expansion after the year 1723*

After Emperor Aurangzeb's death in 1707, Shahuji, son of Sambhaji (and grandson of Shivaji), was released by Azam Shah, the next Mughal emperor, under conditions that rendered him a vassal of the Mughal emperor but his mother was still held captive to ensure good behaviour from Shahuji. He immediately claimed the Maratha throne and challenged his aunt Tarabai and her son. This promptly turned the now-spluttering Mughal-Maratha war into a three-cornered affair. The states of Satara and Kolhapur came into being in 1707, because of the succession dispute over the Maratha kingship. By 1710, two separate principalities had become an established fact, eventually confirmed by the Treaty of Warna in 1731.

In 1713 Farrukhsiyar declared himself Mughal emperor. His bid for power depended heavily on two brothers, known as the Saiyids, one of whom was the governor of Allahabad and the other the governor of Patna.

However, the brothers had a falling-out with the emperor. Negotiations between the Saiyids and Peshwa Balaji Vishwanath, a civilian representative of Shahu, drew the Marathas into the vendetta against the emperor.

In 1714, an army of Marathas commanded by Parsoji Bhosale marched up to Delhi unopposed and managed to depose the Mughal emperor. In return for this help, Balaji Vishwanath managed to negotiate a substantial treaty. Shahuji would have to accept Mughal rule in the Deccan, furnish forces for the imperial army, and pay an annual tribute.

But in return, he received a firman, or imperial directive, guaranteeing himSwaraj, or independence, in the Maratha homeland, plus rights to chauth and sardeshmukh (amounting to 35 percent of the total revenue) throughout Gujarat, Malwa, and the now six provinces of the Mughal Deccan. This treaty also released Yesubai, Shahuji's mother, from Mughal prison.

During regime of Shahu, Raghuji Bhosale expanded the empire in East reaching present-day Bangladesh. Senapati Dabhade expanded in West. Peshwa Bajirao and his three chiefs Pawar (Dhar), Holkar (Indore) and Shinde (Gwalior) expanded in North. These all houses became hereditary, thereby undermining kings authority in due course of time.

### The Peshwa Era (1749 to 1761)

*Fig.: Shaniwarwada palace fort in Pune, it was the seat of the Peshwa rulers of the Maratha Empire until 1818*

During this era, Peshwas controlled the Maratha army and later became the hereditary rulers of the Maratha Empire from 1749 to 1818. During their rein, the Maratha Empire reached its zenith ruling most of the Indian Subcontinent. Prior to 1700, one Peshwa received the status of imperial regent for eight or nine years. They oversaw the greatest expansion of the Maratha Empire around 1760 with the help ofSardars like Holkar, Scindia, Bhosale, Pantpratinidhi, Gaekwad (Dhane), Panse, actually caused a social revolution by bringing capable people into power irrespective of their social status. This was an indication of a great social mobility within the Maratha Empire, enabling its rapid expansion.

Shrimant Baji Rao Vishwanath Bhatt (August 18, 1699 - April 25, 1740), also known as Baji Rao I, was a noted general who served as Peshwa (Prime Minister) to the fourth Maratha Chhatrapati (Emperor) Shahu between 1719 until death. During his lifetime, he never lost a battle. He is credited with expanding the Maratha Empire especially in north that reached its zenith twenty years after his death. PeshwaBajirao fought over 41 battles and is reputed to have never lost one.

Battle of Palkhed was a land battle that took place on February 28, 1728 at the village of Palkhed, near the city of Nashik, Maharashtra, India between Baji Rao I and the Nizam-ul-Mulk of Hyderabad. The Marathas defeated the Nizam. The battle is considered an example of brilliant execution of military strategy.

The Battle of Vasai was fought between the Marathas and the Portuguese rulers of Vasai, a village lying near Mumbai in the present-day state of Maharashtra, India. The Marathas were led by Chimaji Appa, a brother of Peshwa Baji Rao I. Maratha victory in this war was a major achievement of Baji Rao I reign. Standing tall, poised and confident before Shahu Maharaj and his court, the young new Peshwa Baji Rao is said to have thundered:

"Let us transcend the barren Deccan and conquer central India. The Mughals have become weak indolent womanizers andopium-addicts. The accumulated wealth of centuries in the vaults of the north, can be ours. It is time to drive from the holy land of Bharatvarsha the

Vinchurkar, Pethe, Raste, Phadke, Patwardhan, Pawar, Pandit and Purandare, until its eventual annexation by the British East India Company in 1818.

## Ramchandra Pant Amatya Bawdekar

Ramchandra Pant Amatya Bawdekar was a court administrator who rose from the ranks of a local Kulkarni to the ranks of Ashtapradhan under guidance and support of Shivaji. He was one of the prominent Peshwas from the time of Shivaji, prior to the rise of the later Peshwas who controlled the empire after Shahuji. When Chhatrapati Rajaram fled to Jinji in 1689 leaving Maratha Empire, he gave a "Hukumat Panha" (King Status) to Pant before leaving.

Ramchandra Pant managed the entire state under many challenges like influx of Mughals, betrayal from Vatandars (local satraps under the Maratha state) and social challenges like scarcity of food. With the help of Pantpratinidhi, Sachiv, he kept the economic condition of Maratha Empire in an appropriate state.

He received military help from the Maratha commanders – Santaji Ghorpade and Dhanaji Jadhav. On many occasions he himself participated in battles against Mughals and played the role of shadow ruler in absence of Chhatrapati Rajaram. In 1698, he happily stepped down from the post of "Hukumat Panha" when Rajaram offered this post to his wife, Tarabai. Tarabai gave an important position to Pant among senior administrators of Maratha State. He wrote "Adnyapatra" in which he has explained different techniques of war, maintenance of forts and administration etc. But owing to his loyalty to Tarabai against Shahuji (who was supported by more local satraps), he was sidelined after arrival of Shahuji in 1707.

*Baji Rao I*

*Fig.: Baji Rao I*

After Balaji Vishwanath's death in April, 1719, his son, Baji Rao I was appointed as Peshwa by Chattrapati Shahuji, one of the most liberal emperors. Shahuji possessed a strong capacity for recognising talent, and

outcaste and the barbarian. Let us throw them back over the Himalayas, back to where they came from. The Maratha flag must fly from the Krishna to the Indus. Hindustan is ours."

### Balaji Baji Rao

Baji Rao's son, Balaji Bajirao (Nanasaheb), was appointed as a Peshwa by Shahuji. The period between 1741 and 1745 was one of comparative calm in the Deccan. Shahuji died in 1749 bequething power to peshwa with condition that the dignity of house of shivaji will be maintained and also welfare of subjects will be looked after.

In 1740, the Maratha forces came down upon Arcot and invaded the Nawab of Arcot, Dost Ali in the pass of Damalcherry. In the war that followed, Dost Ali, one of his sons Hasan Ali, and a number of prominent persons lost their lives. This initial success at once enhanced Maratha prestige in the south. From Damalcherry the Marathas proceeded to Arcot. It surrendered to them without much resistance. Then, Raghuji invested Trichinopoly in December 1740. Unable to resist, Chanda Saheb delivered the fort to Raghuji on 14 March 1741, on the day of Ram Navami. Chanda Saheb and his son were arrested and sent to Nagpur.

After the successful campaign of Karnatak and Battle of Trichinopolly, Raghuji returned from Karnatak. He undertook six expeditions in Bengal from 1741-1748. Raghuji was able to annex Orissa to his kingdom permanently as he successfully exploited the chaotic conditions prevailing in Bengal, Bihar and Orissa after the death of their Governor Murshid Quli Khan in 1727. Constantly harassed by the Bhonsles, Orissa or Katak,

Bengal and parts of Bihar were economically ruined. Alivardi Khan, Nawab of Bengal made peace with Raghuji in 1751 ceding in perpetuity Katak up to the river Suvarnarekha, and agreeing to pay Rs. 12 lacs annually in lieu of the Chauth of Bengal and Bihar.

*Fig.: Maratha Court*

The smaller States of Raipur, Ratanpur, Bilaspur and Sambalpur belonging to Chhattisgad territory were conquered by Bhaskar Ram, and were placed in charge of Mohansingh, an illegitimate son of Raghuji. Towards the end of his career, Raghuji had conquered the whole of Berar; the Gond kingdoms of Devgad including Nagpur, Gadha-Mandla and Chandrapur; the Subha of Katak; and the smaller states spreading between Nagpur and Katak.

Nanasaheb encouraged agriculture, protected the villagers, and brought about a marked improvement in the state of the territory. Continued expansion saw Raghunath Rao, the brother of Nanasaheb, pushing into in the wake of the Afghan withdrawal after Ahmed Shah Abdali's plunder of Delhi in 1756. In Lahore, as in Delhi, the Marathas were now major players.

Raghoba's letter to Peshwa Balaji Bajirao, 4 May 1758:

*"Lahore, Multan, Kashmir and other subhas on this side of Attock are under our rule for the most part, and places which have not come under our rule we shall soon bring under us. Ahmad Shah Durrani's son Timur Shah Durrani and Jahan Khan have been pursued by our troops, and their troops completely looted. Both of them have now reached Peshawar with a few broken troops. So Ahmad Shah Durrani has returned to Kandahar with some 12-14 thousand broken troops. Thus all have risen against Ahmad who has lost control over the region. We have decided to extend our rule up to Kandahar."*

On 8 May 1758, the Marathas captured Peshawar, defeating the Afghan troops in the Battle of Peshawar. In 1759, The Marathas underSadashivrao Bhau (referred to as the Bhau or Bhao in sources) responded to the news of the Afghans' return to North India by sending a big army to North. Bhau's force was bolstered by some Maratha forces under Holkar, Scindia, Gaikwad and Govind Pant Bundela.

The combined army of over 100,000 regular troops had captured the Mughal capital, Delhi, from an Afghan garrison in December 1759. Delhi had been reduced to ashes many times due to previous invasions, and in addition there being acute shortage of supplies in the Maratha camp. Bhau ordered the sacking of the already depopulated city. He is said to have planned to place his nephew and the Peshwa's son, Vishwasrao, on the Mughal throne.

By 1760, with defeat of the Nizam in the Deccan, Maratha power had reached its zenith with a territory of over 2,800,000 km² acres. Ahmad Shah Durrani, then called Rohillas and Nawab of Oudh to assist him in driving out 'infidel' Marathas from Delhi.

Huge armies of Muslim forces and Marathas collided with each other on 14 January 1761 in the Third Battle of Panipat. The Maratha army lost the battle which halted imperial expansion. The Jats and Rajputs did not support the Marathas. Their withdrawal from the ensuing battle played a crucial role in its result.

The Marathas had antagonised the Jats and Rajputs by taxing them heavily, punishing them after defeating the Mughals and interfering in their internal affairs. The Marathas were abandoned by Raja Suraj Mal of Bharatpur and the Rajputs who quit the Maratha alliance at Agra before the start of the great battle and withdrew their troops, as Maratha generalSadashivrao Bhau did not heed the advice to leave soldier's families (women and children) and pilgrims at Agra and not take them to the battle field with the soldiers, rejected their cooperation. Their supply chains (earlier assured by Raja Suraj Mal and Rajputs) did not exist.

*The Confederacy era (1761-1818)*

*Fig.: Mahadaji Sindhia*

During this period various chiefs and statesman became de facto ruler. The Peshwa was relegated to secondary position. He also became ceremonial king especially after death of Peshwa Madhavrao I. After 1761, young Madhavrao Peshwa tried his best to rebuild the empire in spite of his frail health and reinstated the Maratha authority over North India, 10 years after the battle of Panipat.

In a bid to effectively manage the large empire, semi-autonomy was given to strongest of the knights. Thus, the autonomous Maratha states came into being in far flung regions of the empire:

- Peshwas of Pune
- Gaekwads of Baroda
- Pawars of Dhar
- Holkars of Indore and Malwa
- Scindias of Gwalior and Ujjain
- Bhonsales of Nagpur (no blood relation with Shivaji's or Tarabai's family)
- Even in the Maharashtra itself many knights were given semi-autonomous charges of small districts, which led to princely states like Sangli, Aundh, Bhor, Bawda, Jat, Phaltan, Miraj etc. Pawars of Udgir were also part of confederacy.

Mahadaji Sindhia was the Maratha ruler of the state of Gwalior in central India. Mahadaji was instrumental in resurrecting Maratha power after the debacle of the Third Battle of Panipat in 1761, and rose to become a trusted lieutenant of the Peshwa, leader of the Maratha Empire, as well as the Mughal emperor Shah Alam II.

He took full advantage of the system of neutrality pursued by the British to resurrect Maratha power over Northern India. In this he was assisted by Benoît de

Boigne who increased Sindhia's regular forces to three brigades. With these troops Sindhia became a power in northern India.

After the growth in power of feudal lords like Malwa sardars, landlords of Bundelkhand and Rajput kingdoms of Rajasthan, they refused to pay tribute to Mahadji. So he sent his army conquer the states such as Bhopal, Datiya, Chanderi (1782), Narwar, Salbai and Gohad. He launched an expedition against the Raja of Jaipur, but withdrew after the inconclusive Battle of Lalsot in 1787.

The strong fort of Gwalior was then in the hands of Chhatar Singh, the Jat ruler of Gohad. In 1783, Mahadji besieged the fort of Gwalior and conquered it. He delegated the administration of Gwalior to Khanderao Hari Bhalerao. After celebrating the conquest of Gwalior, Mahadji Shinde turned his attention to Delhi.

In early 1771, ten years after the collapse of Maratha supremacy in North India following the Third Battle of Panipat, Mahadji recaptured Delhi and installed Shah Alam II as the puppet ruler on the Mughal throne receiving in return the title of deputy Vakil-ul-Mutlak or vice-regent of the Empire and that of Vakil-ul-Mutlak being at his request conferred on the Peshwa.

The Mughals also gave him the title of Amir-ul-Amara (head of the amirs). Mahadji ruled the Punjab as it was a Mughal territory and Sikh sardars and other Rajas of the cis-Sutlej region paid tributes to him. The Battle of Gajendragad was fought between the Marathas under the command of Tukojirao Holkar (the adopted son of Malharrao Holkar) and Tipu Sultan from March 1786 to March 1787 in which Tipu Sultan was defeated by the

Marathas. By the victory in this battle, the border of the Maratha territory extended till Tungabhadra River.

In 1788 Mahadji's armies defeated Ismail Beg, a Mughal noble who resisted the Marathas. The Rohilla chief Ghulam Kadir, Ismail Beg's ally, took over Delhi, capital of the Mughal Empire, and deposed and blinded the Emperor Shah Alam II, placing a puppet on the Delhi throne. Mahadji intervened, taking possession of Delhi on October 2, restoring Shah Alam to the throne and acting as his protector. Mahadji sent de Boigne to crush the forces of Jaipur at Patan (June 20, 1790) and the armies of Marwar at Merta on September 10, 1790.

Another achievement of Mahadji was his victory over the Nizam of Hyderabad's army in a battle. The Nizam ceased be a factor in the north Indian politics after this battle and it generally confined itself in the Deccan afterwards. After the peace made with Tipu Sultan of Mysore in 1792, Mahadji successfully exerted his influence to prevent the completion of a treaty between the British, the Nizam of Hyderabad, and the Peshwa, directed against Tipu.

### British Intervention

In 1775, the British East India Company, from its base in Bombay, intervened in a succession struggle in Pune, on behalf ofRaghunathrao (also called Raghobadada), which became the First Anglo-Maratha War. That ended in 1782 with a restoration of the pre-war status quo. Marathas under Tukojirao Holkar and Mahadaji Shinde had defeated British in the battle of Vadgaon. In 1802 the British intervened in Baroda to support the heir to the throne against rival claimants, and they signed a treaty with the new Maharaja recognizing his independence from the Maratha Empire in return for his acknowledgement of British paramountcy. In the Second Anglo-Maratha War (1803–1805), the Peshwa Baji Rao II signed a similar treaty.

In 1799, Yashwantrao Holkar was crowned King, he captured Ujjain. He started campaigning towards the north to expand his empire in that region. Yashwant Rao rebelled against the policies of the Peshwa Baji Rao II.

On May 1802, he marched towardsPune the seat of the Peshwa. This gave rise to the Battle of Poona in which the Peshwa was defeated. After the Battle of Poona, the flight of Peshwa left the government of Maratha state in the hands of Yashwantrao Holkar. He appointed Amrutrao as the Peshwa and went to Indore on 13 March 1803.

All except Gaikwad chief of Baroda, who had already accepted British protection by a separate treaty on 26 July 1802, supported the new regime. He made a treaty with the British in 1805, that fulfilled his demands. Also, Yashwant-Rao successfully resolved the disputes with Scindia and the Peshwa. He tried to unite the Maratha Confederacy but to no avail. Ultimately the Third Anglo-Maratha War (1817–1818), a last-ditch effort to regain sovereignty, resulted in the loss of Maratha independence: it left the British in control of most of India.

The Peshwa was exiled to Bithoor (Maratnear Kanpur, Uttar Pradesh) as a pensioner of the British. The Maratha heartland of Desh, including Pune, came under direct British rule, with the exception of the states of Kolhapur and Satara, which retained local Maratha rulers. The Maratha-ruled states of Gwalior, Indore, and Nagpur all lost territory, and came under subordinate alliance with the British Raj as princely states that retained internal sovereignty under British 'paramountcy'. Other small princely states of Maratha knights were retained under the British Raj as well.

At the end of the war, all of the Maratha powers had surrendered to the British. Shinde, which resulted in the Treaty of Gwailor on 5 November 1817. Under this treaty, Shinde surrendered Rajasthan to the British and agreed to help them fight the Pindaris.

Holkar was defeated on 21 December 1817 and signed the Treaty of Mandeswar on 6 January 1818. Under this treaty the Holkar state became subsidiary to the British. The young Malhar Rao was raised to the throne.Bhonsle was defeated on 26 November 1817 and was captured but he escaped to live out his life inJodhpur.

The Peshwa surrendered on 3 June 1818 and was sent off to Bithur near Kanpur under the terms of the treaty signed on 3 June 1818. Of the Pindari leaders, Karim Khan surrendered to Malcolm in February 1818; Wasim Mohammad surrendered to Shinde and eventually poisoned himself; and Setu was killed by a tiger. The war left the British, under the auspices of the British East India Company, in control of virtually all of present-day India south of the Sutlej River. The famed Nassak Diamond was acquired by the Company as part of the spoils of the war. The British acquired large chunks of territory from the Maratha Empire and in effect put an end to their most dynamic opposition.

The terms of surrender Malcolm offered to the Peshwa were controversial amongst the British for being too liberal: The Peshwa was offered a luxurious life near Kanpur and given a pension of about 80,000 pounds. A comparison was drawn with Napoleon, who was confined to a small rock in the south Atlantic and given a small sum for his maintenance. Trimbakji Dengale was captured after the war and was sent to the fortress of Chunar in Bengal where he spent the rest of his life. With all active resistance over, John Malcolm played a prominent part in capturing and pacifying the remaining fugitives.

## *Maharaja Yashwantrao Holkar*

*Fig.: Maharaja Yashwantrao Holkar in 1802*

After the Battle of Poona, the flight of Peshwa left the government of Maratha state in the hands of Yashwantrao Holkar. He appointed Amrutrao as the Peshwa and went to Indore on 13 March 1803. All except Gaikwad chief of Baroda, who had already accepted British protection by a separate treaty on 26 July 1802, supported the new regime. He made a treaty with the British in 1805, that fulfilled his demands. Also, Yashwant-Rao successfully resolved the disputes with Scindia and the Peshwa. His battles were the most remarkable in the military history of India and the title given to him by the Mughal Emperor gave him a prominent position amongst the rulers of India.

He tried to unite the Maratha Confederacy. In a letter dated 15 February 1806 to Vyankoji Bhosale of Nagpur he states:

*"The Maratha state had been grasped by foreigners. To resist their aggression, God knows, how during the last two and a half years I sacrificed everything, fighting night and day, without a moment's rest. I paid a visit to Daulatrao Sindia and explained to him how necessary it was for all of us to join in averting foreign domination. But Daulatrao failed me. It was mutual cooperation and goodwill which enabled our ancestors to build up, the Maratha states. But now we have all become self-seekers. You wrote to me that you were coming for my support, but you did not make your promise good. If you had advanced into Bengal as was planned, we could have paralyzed the British Government. It is no use of now talking of past things. When I found myself abandoned on all sides, I accepted the offer which the British agents brought to me and concluded the war."*

He was as clever organizer as he was skillful in war. The various branches of the army were organized on a sound military basis. As a military strategist he ranks among the foremost generals who have ever trod on Indian soil.

His heroic achievements shed a noble luster on his military genius, political sagacity and indefatigable industry. He was undoubtedly the greatest and most romantic figure on the stage of Indian history.

Yashwant Rao Holkar rose to power from initial nothingness entirely by dint of his personal valour and spirit of adventure. So great was his personality that even in those troublesome times, no state or power could venture to commit aggression on his territory; and this influence kept the Holkar State secure even after his death for some years.

*Administration*

*Fig.: Engraving of a Maratha Soldier by Alken Henry.*

**Fig.:** *Engraving of a Maratha Soldier by James Forbes 1813*

The organization of Marathas' administration was composed of several ministers (pradhaanas):

- *Peshwa:* Mukhya (main) Pradhan, Prime Minister to the Emperor, for supervising and governing in his absence. The Emperor's orders bore the Peshwa's seal.

- *Mutalik:* Deputy to the Peshwa, Deputy Prime Minister to the Emperor.

- *Rajadnya:* Deputy to the Crown.
- *Sardar Senapati or Sarnaubat:* To manage military forces and administer lands (e.g., Sarsenapati Ghorpade).
- *Sardar:* To manage military forces and administer lands.
- *Mazumdar:* An auditor to manage receipts and expenditures, keep the Crown informed of finances and sign district-level accounts.
- *Amatya:* Chief Mazumdar (Chief Revenue Minister) (e.g., Ramchandra Pant Amatya).
- *Navis or Waqia Mantri:* to record daily activities of the royal family and to serve as the master of ceremonies.
- *Sur Navis or Sacheev:* Imperial Secretary, to oversee the Crown's correspondence to ensure letter and style adherence (e.g., Shankaraji Narayan Sacheev).
- *Sumant or Dabir:* Foreign Minister, to manage foreign affairs and receive ambassadors.
- *Pandit:* to adjudicate internal religious disputes and promote formal education and spiritual practice (e.g., Melgiri Pandit).
- Nyayadhish: the highest judicial authority (Chief Justice).

Peshwa was the titular equivalent of a modern Prime Minister. Emperor Shivaji created the Peshwa designation in order to more effectively delegate administrative duties during the growth of the Maratha Empire. Prior to 1749, Peshwas held office for 8–9 years and controlled the

Maratha army. They later became the de facto hereditary administrators of the Maratha Empire from 1749 till its end in 1818.

Under Peshwa administration and with the support of several key generals and diplomats, the Maratha Empire reached its zenith, ruling most of the Indian subcontinent landmass. It was also under the Peshwas that the Maratha Empire came to its end through its formal annexation into the British Empire by the British East India Company in 1818. The Marathas used secular policy of administration and allowed complete freedom of religion. There were many notable Muslims in the military and administration of Marathas like Ibrahim Khan Gardi, Haider Ali Kohari, Daulat Khan, Siddi Ibrahim, Jiva Mahal etc.

Shivaji was an able administrator who established a government that included modern concepts such as cabinet, foreign affairs andinternal intelligence. He established an effective civil and military administration. He believed that there was a close bond between the state and the citizens. He is remembered as a just and welfare-minded king. Cosme da Guarda says about Shivaji in 'Life of the Celebrated Sevaji':

"Such was the good treatment Shivaji accorded to people and such was the honesty with which he observed the capitulations that none looked upon him without a feeling of love and confidence. By his people he was exceedingly loved. Both in matters of reward and punishment he was so impartial that while he lived he made no exception for any person; no merit was left unrewarded, no offence went unpunished; and this he did with so much care and attention that he specially charged his governors to inform him in writing of the conduct of his soldiers, mentioning in particular those who had distinguished themselves, and he would at once order their promotion, either in rank or in pay, according to their merit. He was naturally loved by all men of valor and good conduct."

However, the later Marathas are remembered more for their military campaigns, not for their administration. Hindu historians have criticized the treatment of Marathas with Jats andRajputs. Historian K Roy writes:

"The treatment of Marathas with their co-religionist fellows - Jats and Rajputs was definitely unfair, and ultimately they had to pay its price in Panipat where Muslim forces had united in the name of religion."

Maratha Empire, at its peak, ruled over much of the Indian Subcontinent (modern-day Republic of India, Pakistan and Bangladesh as well as bordering Nepal and Afghanistan). Apart from capturing various regions, the Marathas maintained a large number of tributaries who were bounded by agreement to pay a certain amount of annual tax, known as "Chauth". Apart from capturing the whole Mughal Empire, the Maratha Empire defeatedSultanate of Mysore under Hyder Ali and Tipu Sultan, Nawab of Oudh, Nawab of Bengal, Nizam of Hyderabad and Nawab of Arcot as well as thePolygar kingdoms of South India. They extracted chauth from Delhi, Oudh, Bengal, Bihar, Orissa, Punjab, Hyderabad, Mysore, Uttar Pradesh andRajput states.

In 1758, the Maratha Empire expanded its boundary till Afghanistan. They defeated Afghan forces in what is now Pakistan as well as Kashmir. The Afghans were numbered around 25,000-30,000 and were led by Timur

Shah, the son of Ahmad Shah Durrani. In April 1758, the Marathas massacred and looted thousands of Afghan soldiers and captured Lahore, Multan, Peshawar, Attock in the Punjab region and Kashmir. The Marathas were requested by Safdarjung, the Nawab of Oudh, in 1752 to help him defeat Afghani Rohilla. The Maratha force left Poona and defeated Afghan Rohilla in 1752, capturing the whole of Rohilkhand (present-day northwestern Uttar Pradesh).

During the confederacy area, Mahadji Sindhia resurrected the Maratha domination on North India, which was lost after the Third battle of Panipat, at the time of British Military intevention much of North India, including modern day east Punjab & Haryana including the The Cis-Sutlej states(south of Sutlej) like Kaithal, Patiala, Jind, Thanesar, Maler Kotla, and Faridkot, Delhi and UP were under the suzeranity of the Scindhia dynasty of the Maratha Empire, following the Second Anglo-Maratha War of 1803-1805, Marathas lost these territories to the British.

The Maratha Empire is credited with laying the foundation of the Indian Navy and bringing about considerable changes in naval warfare by introducing a blue-water navy. The Maratha Empire is also credited for developing many important cities like Pune, Baroda, and Indore. From its inception in 1674, the Marathas established a Naval force, consisting of cannons mounted on ships.

The dominance of the Maratha Navy started with the ascent of Kanhoji Angre as the Darya-Saranga by the Maratha chief of Satara.Under that authority, he was admiral of the Western coast of India from Mumbai to

Vingoria (now Vengurla) in the present day state ofMaharashtra, except for Janjira which was affiliated with the Mughal Empire. Until his death in 1729, he repeatedly attacked the colonial powers of Britain and Portugal, capturing numerous vessels of the British East India Company and extracting ransom for their return.

On 29 November 1721, a joint attempt by the Portuguese Viceroy Francisco José de Sampaio e Castro and the British General Robert Cowan to humble Kanhoji failed miserably.

Their combined fleet consisted of 6,000 soldiers in no less than four Man-of-war besides other ships led by Captain Thomas Mathews of the Bombay Marine failed miserably.

Aided by Maratha naval commanders Mendhaji Bhatkar and Mainak Bhandari, Kanhoji continued to harass and plunder the European ships until his death in 1729.

The 'Pal' was a three masted Maratha man-of-war with guns peeping on the broadsides.

Personalities:

- Chhatrapati Shivaji Maharaj (1630–1680)
- Chhatrapati Sambhaji (1657–1689)
- Chhatrapati Rajaram (1670–1700)
- Maharani Tarabai (1675–1761)
- Chhatrapati Shahu (1682–1749) (alias Shivaji II, son of Chhatrapati Sambhaji)
- Chhatrapati Ramaraja (nominally, grandson of Chhatrapati Rajaram and Queen Tarabai)

Kolhapur:

- Queen Tarabai (1675–1761) (wife of Chhatrapati Rajaram) in the name of her son Shivaji II
- Chhatrapati Sambhaji (son of Chhatrapati Rajaram from his second wife)
- Chhatrapati Shahu IV

Peshwas:

- Sonopant Dabir (1640–1652)
- Shyampant Kulkarni-Ranzekar (1652–1657)
- Moropant Trimbak Pingle (1657–1683)
- Moreshwar Pingale (1683–1689)
- RamchandraPant Amatya (1689–1708)
- Bahiroji Pingale (1708–1711)
- Parshuram Tribak Kulkarni (1711–1713)
- Balaji Vishwanath (1713–1720)
- Peshwa Bajirao I (1720–1740)
- Balaji Bajirao (4 Jul.1740-23 Jun.1761) (b. 8 Dec.1721, d. 23 Jun.1761)
- Madhavrao Peshwa (1761-18 Nov.1772) (b. 16 Feb. 1745, d. 18 Nov. 1772)
- Narayanrao Bajirao (13 Dec.1772-30 Aug.1773) (b. 10 Aug.1755, d. 30 Aug.1773)
- Raghunathrao (5 Dec.1773–1774) (b. 18 Aug.1734, d. 11 Dec.1783)
- Sawai Madhava Rao II Narayan (1774-27 Oct.1795) (b. 18 Apr.1774, d. 27 Oct.1795)

- Chimnajee Madhavarao (26 May 1796 – 6 Dec 1796) (brother of Bajirao II, adopted by Madhavrao II's wife)

- Baji Rao II (6 Dec.1796 - 3 Jun.1818) (d. 28 Jan.1851)

- Amritrao (brother of Bajirao II), Peshwa for a short period during Yashwantrao Holkar's Rule (May 1802 – May 1803).

- Nana Sahib (1 Jul.1857–1858) (b. 19 May.1825, d. 24 Sep.1859)

Chieftains:

- Holkar

- Shinde (Scindia)

- Gaikwad

- Bhonsale (Nagpur)

Shivaji was born in the hill-fort of Shivneri, near the Junnar city in Pune district. On the auspicious second day of the bright half of Vaishakh, in the year 1549 of Shaka era (1627 A.D.) to the sound pipes and drums playing in the 'Nagar Khana', Jijabai gave birth to a son. On the twelfth day, with the ceremony, the child was named 'Shivaji' after goddess Shivadevi whose temple was in the fort.

His exact date of birth has been a matter of dispute among the various historians in the past. The Maharashtra state government now accepts the 3rd day of the dark half of Phalguna, year 1551 of Shaka calendar (Friday, 19 February 1630) as the true birthdate of Shivaji. Other suggested dates include 6 April 1627, or other dates near this day.

Shivaji's father Shahaji Bhosale was the leader of a band of mercenaries that serviced the Deccan Sultanates. His mother was Jijabai, the daughter of Lakhujirao Jadhav of Sindkhed.

*Fig.: Shivaji with Jijamata.*

During the period of Shivaji's birth, the power in Deccan was shared by three Islamic sultanates – Bijapur,

Ahmednagar, and Golconda. Shahaji kept changing his loyalty between the Nizamshahi of Ahmadnagar, Adil Shah of Bijapur and the Mughals, but always kept his *jagir* (fiefdom) at Pune and his small army with him.

Following a treaty between the Mughals and the Bijapur Sultanate, Shahaji was posted to Bangalore-based jagir, while Jijabai and Shivaji remained in Pune.

Shivaji was extremely devoted to his mother Jijabai, who was deeply religious. This religious environment had a profound influence on Shivaji, and he carefully studied the two great Hindu epics, Ramayana and Mahabharata.

The morality and spiritual messages of the epics made a great impression on him.

Throughout his life he was deeply interested in religious teachings, and sought the company of Hindu and Sufi (an esoteric Muslim sect) saints throughout his life.

Shivaji drew his earliest trusted comrades and a large number of his soldiers from the Maval region, including Yesaji Kank, Suryaji Kakade, Baji Pasalkar, Baji Prabhu Deshpande and Tanaji Malusare.

In the company of his Maval comrades, a young Shivaji wandered over the hills and forests of the Sahyadri range, hardening himself and acquiring first-hand knowledge of the land. By 1639, he commanded a hardy and loyal band of officers and soldiers.

At the age of 12, Shivaji was taken to Bangalore where he was further formally trained along-with elder brother Sambhaji and stepbrother Ekoji I. He married Saibai, a member of the prominent Nimbalkar family in 1640. At age of 14, he returned to Pune with a *rajmudra* (sovereign seal) and council of minister.

## Confrontation with the Regional Sultanate of Adilshah

In 1645, at the age of 16, Shivaji managed to pursue the Bijapuri commander of the Torna Fort, named Inayat Khan, to hand over the possession of the fort to him.

Firangoji Narsala, who held the Chakan fort professed his loyalty to him and the fort of Kondana was acquired by bribing the Adil-Shahi governor.

On 25 July 1648, Shahaji was imprisoned by Baji Ghorpade under the orders of Adilshah in a bid to contain Shivaji.

Adilshah also sent an army led by Farradkhan against Shahji's other son Sambhaji at Bangalore, and another army led by Fattekhan against Shivaji at Purandhar. Both Bhosale brothers defeated the invading armies.

## Battle of Purander

An army led by Fattekhan was defeated by Shivaji in the battle of Purandhar.

Meanwhile, Shivaji had petitioned Emperor Shahjahan's son, Murad Baksh, who was governor of Deccan, pledging his loyalty to the Mughals to seek his support in securing the release of his father.

The Mughals recognised Shivaji as a Mughal *sardar* and pressured Adilshah to release Shahaji.

On 16 May 1649 Shahaji was released after Shivaji and Sambhaji surrendering the forts of Kondhana, Bangalore and Kandarpi.

## Battle of Pratapgad

*Fig.: Death of Afzal Khan*

In 1659, Adilshah sent Afzal Khan, an experienced and veteran general to destroy Shivaji in an effort to put down what he saw as a regional revolt. Afzal Khan desecrated Hindu temples at Tuljapur and Pandharpur hoping to draw Shivaji to the plains to retaliate with his limited military resources and thus lead him and his budding military power to easy destruction by the numerically bigger, better-armed and more professional Bijapur army.

Afzal Khan may have expected Shivaji to meet his army in the plains, however Shivaji, upon carefully weighing his options, agreed to meet Afzal Khan on his home turf on pretext of diplomatic negotiations. Shivaji sent a letter to Afzal Khan stating that he was eager for a meeting. The meeting was arranged between Afzal Khan and Shivaji at the foothills of Pratapgad Fort on the day 10 November 1659 Pratapgad.

This event is one of the most important in Shivaji's life. Shivaji got a pledge from ministers to never submit in case he fell. It is said that during this period, Shivaji had a vision of Goddess Bhavani promising full protection on the confrontation and victory.

Afzal Khan was invited to a hut at the base of Pratapgad under the conditions that both the men would be armed only with a sword and attended by a follower. However, Shivaji is said to have learnt that Afzal Khan was planning an attack on him.

Shivaji, therefore, wore armour underneath his clothes and concealed a Bagh nakh in his left arm, in addition to a visibile dagger on his right hand. Accounts vary on whether Shivaji or Afzal Khan struck the first blow: the Maratha chronicles accuse Afzal Khan of treachery, while the Persian-language chronicles attribute the treachery to Shivaji. Ultimately, Afzal Khan was disemboweled by Shivaji and later decapitated by Sambhaji Kavji.

*Fig.: Pratapgad fort*

In the ensuing Battle of Pratapgarh fought on 10 November 1659, Shivaji's forces decisively defeated the

Bijapur Sultanate's forces. It was their first significant military victory against a major regional power, and led to the eventual establishment of the Maratha Empire. The Maratha troops led by Kanhoji Jedhe attacked Afzal Khan's Bijapuri forces and routed them at the foothills of the fort. Then in a rapid march, a section of Adilshahi forces commanded by Musekhan was attacked. Musekhan was wounded and subsequently fled, abandoning his soldiers who were then set upon and decimated by the Marathas.

Commander Moropant Pingale led the infantry in a lighting attack on to the left flank of the Adilshahi troops. Adilshah's artillery was rendered ineffective by the suddenness of this attack at close quarters. At the same time commander Ragho Atre swiftly attacked Adilshahi cavalry before it was fully prepared for battle and almost completely wiped it out. Shivaji's cavalry headed by Netaji Palkar rushed towards Wai in hot pursuit of retreating Adilshahi forces who were attempting to join reserve forces stationed there. The retreating forces of Afzal Khan were engaged in battle and were routed. More than 3,000 soldiers of the Bijapur army were killed and two sons of Afzal Khan were taken as prisoners.

This unexpected and unlikely victory made Shivaji a hero of Maratha folklore and a legendary figure among his people. The large quantities of captured weapons, horses, armour and other materials helped to strengthen the nascent and emerging Maratha army. The Mughal emperor Aurangzeb now identified Shivaji as a major threat to the mighty Mughal Empire. Soon thereafter Shivaji, Shahaji and Netaji Palkar (the chief of the Maratha cavalry) decided to attack and defeat the Adilshahi kingdom at Bijapur. But things did not go as planned as

Shahaji's health deteriorated and they were forced to postpone the planned attack. However, Netoji Palkar undertook this mission mounting smaller scale attacks and military harassment of the Adilshahi kingdom.

Subsequently, the Sultan of Bijapur sent an army composed mainly of Afghan mercenaries to subdue and defeat Shivaji before he could substantially expand his army. In the ensuing battle, Bijapur's army was defeated by the Maratha troops. This intense and bloody battle ended in the unconditional surrender of the Bijapuri forces to Shivaji.

### Battle of Kolhapur

To counter the loss at Pratapgad and to defeat the newly emerging Maratha power, another army, this time numbering over 10,000, was sent against Shivaji, commanded by Bijapur's renowned Abyssinian general Rustamjaman.

With a cavalry of 5,000 Marathas, Shivaji attacked them near Kolhapur on 28 December 1659. In a swift movement, Shivaji led a full frontal attack at the center of the enemy forces while other two portions of his cavalry attacked the flanks.

This battle lasted for several hours and at the end Bijapuri forces were soundly defeated and Rustamjaman ignominiously fled the battlefield. Adilshahi forces lost about 2,000 horses and 12 elephants to the Marathas. This victory alarmed the mighty Mughal Empire who now derisively referred to Shivaji as the "Mountain Rat". Aurangzeb the Mughal emperor was now actively preparing to bring the full might and resources of the Mughal Empire to bear down on the potential Maratha threat.

## Siege of Panhala

*Fig.:* M.V. Dhurandhar's painting of Shivaji.

Per the terms of the Mughal-Adilshahi plan, Adil Shah in 1660 sent Siddi Jauhar, an accomplished general to attack Shivaji on his southern borders, preceding the expected major Mughal attack from the north. He ordered his army of 40,000 north to Kolhapur to confront and defeat Shivaji as a part of their grand alliance with the Mughal emperor Aurangzeb. He secured the support of local chieftains such as Jasvantrao Dalvi of Palavani and Suryarao Surve of Sringarpur to defeat Shivaji. At that time, Shivaji was camped at the Panhala fort near present day Kolhapur with 8,000 Marathas.

Siddi Jauhar's army besieged Panhala on 2 March 1660, cutting off supply routes to the fort. Helping with siege were Baji Ghorpade and Siddi Masud from the west, Sadat Khan and Bhai Khan from the north, Rustam Zaman and Bade Khan from the east, Siddi Jauhar and Fazal Khan from the south. Netaji Palkar, the Commander of the Maratha forces was on a mission away from Panhala harassing and attacking Adilshahi territory and was not able to come to the aid of Shivaji. At this point of time, Shaista Khan had moved from Baramati to Shirwal.

Panhala was a formidable fort and Adilshahi army was repulsed repeatedly by effective cannon fire and heavy rock-pelting. Siddi Jauhar approached Henry Revington, the British chief at the Rajapur port to seek long-range and more powerful cannons. Henry decided to help him in return for future favours, and began pounding Panhala fort. In spite of this Marathas continued defending Panhala and persevered in keeping Siddi Jauhar at bay.

Marathas even raided the Adilshahi camp a few times but without much success. However, in one such raid, Tryambak Bhaskar and Kondaji Farzand presented themselves as allies of the British and Adlishahi forces. They came down to the Adilshahi camp and met Henry

Revington and his associates. They managed to kill one British officer and injured Henry. Thereafter, they sabotaged the cannons and made them ineffective. Jauhar, livid at this, tightened the siege further.

Jauhar did not leave any stone unturned to ensure that the siege around Panhala was unyielding, he personally took utmost care that no one in his army was complacent.

He even braved the tumultuous monsoon season and continued the siege even during heaviest downpours. On hearing about the ever tightening siege of Panhala, Netaji Palkar returned from Bijapur and attacked the Adilshahi forces surrounding Panhala. He tried to break the siege but his smaller forces were pushed back by a much larger Adilshahi army.

Thereafter, Shivaji decided to escape to a nearby fort Vishalgad, where he could regroup his soldiers. He then sent misleading messages to Siddi Jauhar indicating that he was willing to negotiate and was looking for accommodation and mutual understanding. With this news, Adilshahi soldiers relaxed somewhat and Shivaji escaped under the cover of a stormy night on 12 July 1660.

Meanwhile Jauhar's soldiers captured a small group of Marathas apparently including Shivaji only to realize he was a look-alike named Shiva Kashid dressed like Shivaji and sent out to create a diversion and facilitate the real Shivaji's escape. Siddi Johar's soldiers realized that the imposter was Shivaji's barber and that Shivaji and his army were headed to Vishalgad, immediately thereafter a massive chase was undertaken to intercept Shivaji and deal with him and his army, once and for all.

## Marathas' Last Stand: The Battle of Pavan Khind

*Fig.: Plaque to commemorate the entrance to Paavankhind*

Observing that enemy cavalry was fast closing in on them, Shivaji sought to avoid defeat and capture. Baji Prabhu Deshpande, a Maratha sardar of Bandal Deshmukh along with 300 soldiers, volunteered to fight to the death to hold back the enemy at Ghod Khind (a mountain pass in Gajapur which is 4 miles (6.4 km) south of Vishalgad) to give Shivaji and the rest of the army a chance to reach the safety of the Vishalgad fort.

In the ensuing Battle of Pavan Khind, Baji Prabhu Deshpande fought relentlessly. He was wounded but he held on and continued the fight until he heard the sound of cannon fire from Vishalgad, signalling Shivaji had safely reached the fort. The result of this intense and heroic battle was the death of 300 Marathas and 3,000 of Adilshah's troops who were engaged in a fierce combat.

The Marathas were heroically committed to this fatal fight to ensure Shivaji's reaching the fort and they held off a larger enemy force for 7 hours using 2 Dand pattas (flexible sword) one in each hand allowing Shivaji to reach the safety of the fort on 13 July 1660.

Thereafter a truce was made between Shivaji and Adilshah through Shahaji Raje. In addition, as the terms of this accord, Panhala Fort was awarded to Siddi Johar. *Ghod Khind* (*khind* meaning "a narrow mountain pass") was renamed *Paavan Khind* (Sacred Pass) in honor of Bajiprabhu Deshpande, Shibosingh Jadhav, Fuloji, people from Bandal community and all other soldiers who fought in Ghod Khind. People from the Bandal community were specially selected by Shivaji while escaping from Panhala for their knowledge of the region, rock climbing skills, and martial qualities.

### Clash with the Mughals

Till 1657, Shivaji maintained peaceful relations with the Mughals. Shivaji offered his assistance to Aurangzeb in conquering Bijapur and in return, he was assured of the formal recognition of his right to the Bijapuri forts and villages under his possession. Shivaji's confrontations with the Mughals began in March 1657, when two officers of Shivaji raided the Mughal territory near Ahmednagar. This was followed by raids in Junnar, with Shivaji carrying off 300,000 huns in cash and 200 horses.

Aurangzeb responded to the raids by sending Nasiri Khan who defeated the forces of Shivaji at Ahmednagar. However, the countermeasures were interrupted by the rainy season and the battle of succession for the Mughal throne following the illness of Shah Jahan.

### Battle of Umberkhind

An Uzbek general, Kartalab Khan, was sent by Shaista Khan on a mission to attack and reduce the number of forts under Shivaji's control in the Konkan region on 3 February 1661. He left his camp near Pune with 30,000 troops. This time the Mughals did not march openly and took circuitous back country routes, as they sought to surprise Shivaji. But, instead, Shivaji surprised them at a pass known as *Umber Khind* (in a dense forest, near present-day Pen), and attacked them from all sides. Marathas hidden in the dense forest executed a well co-ordinated ambush attack on the Mughal army. Shivaji himself took the forward position with an elite cavalry unit. The other three sides were flanked by Shivaji's light infantry.

In a well co-ordinated movement of light infantry and cavalry, Shivaji prevailed over the invaders. A Maratha lady commander, Raibagan, who co-led the Mughal forces, analyzed the situation and realised that defeat was imminent and advised Kartalab Khan to accept defeat and initiate a compromise with Shivaji. Within four hours into the attack the enemy accepted defeat and surrendered all the supplies, arms and assets. The Mughal army

suffered high casualties. The defeated army was allowed
a safe passage. Kartalab Khan and Raibagan were released
with honour in accordance with Shivaji's terms and his
long standing policy towards women and unarmed
civilians.

### Attack on Shaista Khan

Upon the request of *Badi* Begum of Bijapur, Aurangzeb
sent his maternal uncle (brother of late Queen Mumtaz
Mahal) Shaista Khan, with an army numbering over
150,000 along with a powerful artillery division in January
1660 to defeat Shivaji.

Khan was accompanied by eminent commanders like
Turktaj, Hussain, Haider, Naamdar Khan, Kartalab Khan,
Uzbek Khan, Fateh Jung and Rajputs namely Bhau Singh,
Shyam Singh, Rai Singh Sisodiya, Pradyuman and many
more. Khan was an experienced commander who had
defeated Shahaji in the same region in 1636. He was
ordered to attack the Maratha kingdom in conjunction
with Bijapur's army led by Siddi Jauhar. Aurangzeb
ordered Shaista Khan to capture the Maratha kingdom
to add to the empire (he intended to deceive the Adilshah),
after Shivaji's expected defeat by Jauhar in Panhala fort.
Shivaji now prepared to face a combined attack of Mughals
and Adilshahi forces.

Shaista Khan was ordered by Aurangzeb to attack
Shivaji per the Mughal-Adilshahi accord. Shaista Khan,
with his better equipped and provisioned army of 300,000
that was many times the size of the Maratha forces, seized
Pune and the nearby fort of Chakan. At the time, Firangoji
Narsala was the *killedar* (commander) of fort Chakan,
which was defended by 300–350 Maratha soldiers. They
were able to withstand the Mughal attack on the fort for

one and a half months. Then, a *burj* (outer wall) was blown up with explosives.

This created an opening to the fort allowing hordes of Mughals to breach the exterior portion of the fort. Firangoji, himself, led the Maratha counter attack against a larger Mughal army. Eventually, the fort was lost with the capture of Firangoji, who then was brought before Shaista Khan, who, appreciating his bravery, offered him a *jahagir* (military commission) on the condition that he join the Mughal forces, which Firangoji declined. Admiring his loyalty, Shaista Khan pardoned Firangoji and set him free. Firangoji returned home and Shivaji awarded him a fort named Bhupalgad.

Shaista Khan pressed his advantage of having a larger, better provisioned and heavily armed Mughal army and made inroads into some of the Maratha territory. Although he held Pune for almost a year, he had little further success. He had set up his residence at Lal Mahal, Shivaji's palace, in the city of Pune.

Shaista Khan kept a tight security in Pune. However, Shivaji planned an attack on Shaista Khan amidst tight security. In April 1663, a wedding party had obtained special permission for a procession; Shivaji planned an attack using the wedding party as cover. The Marathas disguised themselves as the bridegroom's procession and entered Pune. Shivaji, having spent much of his youth in Pune, knew his way around the city and his own palace of Lal Mahal. Chimanaji Deshpande — one of the childhood friends of Shivaji — aided him in this attack and offered his services as a personal bodyguard.

According to Babasaheb Purandare, since the Mughal army also consisted of Maratha soldiers, it was difficult for someone to distinguish between Shivaji's Maratha soldiers and the Maratha soldiers of the Mughal army. Taking advantage of this situation, Shivaji, along with a few of his trusted men, infiltrated the Mughal camp.

After overpowering and slaying of the palace guards, the Marathas broke into the mansion by breaching an outer wall. Chimnaji and Netaji Palkar entered first along with Babaji Deshpande, another of Shivaji's long time loyal associates.

They approached Shaista Khan's quarters. Shivaji then personally confronted Shaista Khan in a face to face attack. Meanwhile, perceiving danger, one of Shaista's wives turned off the lights. Shivaji pursued Shaista Khan and severed three of his fingers with his sword (in the darkness) as he fled through an open window. Shaista Khan narrowly escaped death and lost his son and many of his guards and soldiers in the raid.

Within twenty-four hours of this attack, Shaista Khan left Pune and headed North towards Agra. An angered Aurangzeb transferred him to distant Bengal as a punishment for bringing embarrassment to the Mughals with his ignoble defeat in Pune.

### Siege of Surat

In 1664 Shivaji invaded Surat, an important and wealthy Mughal trading city, and looted it to replenish his now depleted treasury and also as a revenge for the capture and looting of Maratha territory by Shaista Khan. (Surat was again sacked by Shivaji in 1670.)

### Treaty of Purandar

Aurangzeb was enraged and sent Mirza Raja Jai Singh I with an army numbering around 15,000 to defeat Shivaji.

Jai Singh planned and executed his battle strategies so well with his vast army that the Mughal forces under him made significant gains and captured many Maratha forts. Shivaji came to terms with Aurangzeb rather than lose more forts and men.

*Fig.: Raja Jai Singh of Amber receiving Shivaji a day before concluding the Treaty of Purandar.*

In the ensuing treaty of Purander, signed between Shivaji and Jai Singh on 11 June 1665, Shivaji agreed to give up 23 of his forts and pay compensation of 400,000 rupees to the Mughals. He also agreed to let his son Sambhaji become a Mughal Sardar, serve the Mughal court of Aurangzeb and fight with Mughals against Bijapur.

He actually fought alongside Raja Jai Singh's Mughal forces against Bijapur's forces for a few months. His commander, Netaji Palkar, joined Mughals, was rewarded very well for his bravery, converted to Islam, changed his name to Quli Mohammed Khan in 1666 and was sent to the Afghan frontier to fight the restive tribes. He returned to Shivaji's service after ten years in 1676 and was accepted back as a Hindu on Shivaji's advice.

## Arrest in Agra and Escape

In 1666, Aurangzeb invited Shivaji to Agra, along with his nine-year-old son Sambhaji. Aurangzeb's plan was to send Shivaji to Kandahar, modern day Afghanistan to consolidate the Mughal Empire's north-western frontier. However, in the court, on 12 May 1666, Aurangzeb made Shivaji stand behind *mansabdârs* (military commanders) of his court. Shivaji took offense at this seeming insult and stormed out of court and was promptly placed under house arrest, under the watch of Faulad Khan, Kotwal of Agra.

From his spies, Shivaji learned that Aurangzeb planned to move his residence to Raja Vitthaldas's Haveli and then to possibly kill him or send him to fight in the Afghan frontier. As a result Shivaji planned his escape. He feigned almost fatal sickness and requested to send most of his contingent back to the Deccan, thereby ensuring the safety of his army and deceiving Aurangzeb. Thereafter, on his request, he was allowed to send daily shipments of sweets and gifts to saints, fakirs, and temples in Agra as offerings for getting well.

After several days and weeks of sending out boxes containing sweets, Shivaji and his nine year old son Sambhaji hid themselves in two of the boxes and managed to escape on 22 July 1666. Shivaji and his son fled to the Deccan disguised as sadhus (holy men). After the escape, rumours of Sambhaji's death were intentionally spread by Shivaji himself in order to deceive the Mughals and to protect Sambhaji.

Dr. Ajit Joshi presented a different view in a Marathi book *Agryahun Sutka*, concluded that Shivaji most likely disguised himself as a Brahmin priest after performance of religious rites at the *haveli* grounds and escaped by mingling in within the departing priestly entourage of Pandit Kavindra Paramananda.

## Battle of Sinhgad

After this escape, both sides maintained calm and a treaty was concluded for some time. However, it was broken at the end of the year 1670. Shivaji launched a major offensive against Mughals. In a span of four months he recovered a major portion of the territories surrendered to Mughals. During this phase, the valiant Tanaji Malusare won the prestigious fort of Sinhgad in the battle of Sinhgad on 4 Feb 1670, although he lost his life.

## Battle of Vani-dindori

Subsequently, Shivaji sacked Surat for second time in 1670. When Shivaji was returning from Surat, Mughals under Daud Khan tried to intercept him, but were defeated in the Battle of Vani-dindori near present-day Nashik.

## Battle of Salher

Peshwa Moropant Pingale won a number of forts in this area. Senapati Prataprao Gujar defeated Mughals in various campaigns. In order to subdue this Maratha resurgence, Dilerkhan was sent along with Bahlol khan and other generals. During this phase, the combined forces of Moropant and Prataprao defeated the Mughals in the open battle of Salher.

This was the first major battle in which Mughals were defeated by any opponent. This greatly raised the status of Marathas and Shivaji, in particular. Against this background of victories, Shivaji decided to coronate himself, thereby giving sovereignty to the Maratha people. However, a tragedy struck in that Shivaji lost his trusted cavalry general Prataprao in the following battle of Nesari.

## Battle of Nesari

In 1674, Prataprao Gujar, the then Commander-in chief of the Maratha forces, was sent to push back the invading force led by the Adil Shahi general, Bahlol Khan. Prataprao's forces defeated and captured the opposing general in the battle after cutting-off their water supply by encircling a strategically located lake, which prompted Bahlol Khan to sue for peace. In spite of Shivaji's specific warnings against doing so Prataprao released Bahlol Khan who started preparing for a fresh invasion.

*Fig.: Towers of the Raigad Fort*

When Shivaji sent a displeasure letter to Prataprao refusing him audience until Bahlol Khan was re-captured. In the ensuing days, he learnt of Bahlol Khan having camped with 15,000 force at Nesari near Kolhapur. Given the uneven match Prataprao reasoned that there was no point in leading his 1,200 cavalrymen into a suicide charge alone. Other six sardars of distinction followed him to perish with their commander.

The seven Maratha officers were Prataprao Gujar, Visaji Ballal, Dipoji Rautrao, Vithal Pilaji Atre, Krishnaji

Bhaskar, Siddi Hilal and Vithoji Shinde. The loss of Prataprao Gujar was a big loss to the Marathas. Anandrao Mohite managed to the withdraw army to safer areas.

Marathas then avenged the death of their general, by defeating Bahlol Khan and capturing his *jagir* (fiefdom) under the leadership of Anaji and Hambirao Mohite. Shivaji was deeply grieved on hearing of Prataprao's death. He arranged for the marriage of his second son, Rajaram, to the daughter of Prataprao Gujar. Anandrao Mohite became Hambirrao Mohite, the new *sarnaubat* (Commander-in-Chief of the Maratha forces). Shivaji started preparation for coronation. Fort Raigad was newly built by Hiroji Indulkar as a capital of rising Maratha kingdom.

### Coronation

*Fig.: The coronation of Shri Shivaji*

Shivaji was crowned a king in a lavish ceremony at Raigad on 6 June 1674. Gaga Bhatt officially presided over the ceremony, and had a gold vessel filled with the seven sacred waters of the rivers Yamuna, Indus, Ganges, Godavari, Krishna and Kaveri.

He held the vessel over Shivaji's head and chanted the coronation mantras, as the water kept dripping from the several tiny holes in the vessel. After the ablution, Shivaji bowed before Jijamata and touched her feet. Nearly fifty thousand people gathered at Raigad for the ceremonies.

Shivaji was bestowed with the sacred thread *jaanva*, with the Vedas and was bathed in an *abhisheka*. Shivaji then had the title of "Shakakarta" conferred upon him, as well as assumed the title 'Kshatriya Kulavantas' meaning head of Kshatriyas. Further, he preferred Chhatrapati title than Maharaja.

His mother Jijabai died on 18 June 1674, within a few days of the coronation. This was considered a bad omen. Therefore, a second coronation was carried out 24 September 1674, this time according to the Bengal school of Tantricism and presided over by Nischal Puri.

### Conquests in Southern India

In October 1674, the Marathas raided Khandesh. On 17 April 1675 Shivaji captured Phonda from Bijapuris. Karwar was occupied by mid 1675 and Kolhapur in July 1675. There were naval skirmishes with the Siddis of Janjira in November 1675. In early 1676, Peshwa Pingale engaged Raja of Ramnagar in battle en route to Surat. Shivaji raided Athani in March 1676. By the end of 1676, Shivaji besieged Belgaum and Vayem Rayim in current day northern Karnataka.

At the end of 1676, Shivaji launched a wave of conquests in southern India with a massive force of 50,000 (30,000 cavalry and 20,000 infantry). He captured the forts at Vellore and Jinji that belonged to the sultanate of Bijapur and are in modern-day Tamil Nadu. In the run-up to this expedition Shivaji appealed to a sense of Deccani patriotism, that the "Deccan" or Southern India was a homeland that should be protected from outsiders.

His appeal was somewhat successful and he entered into a treaty with the Qutubshah of the Golconda sultanate that covered the eastern Deccan. Shivaji's conquests in the south proved quite crucial during future wars. Jinji served as Maratha capital for nine years during the War of 27 years. The small bands of marathas were now moving like imperial forces ready for open battle.

His other intention was to reconcile with his stepbrother Vyankoji (his father Shahaji's son from his second wife, who came from the Mohite family) who ruled Thanjavur after Shahaji. They had talks, Venkoji (Ekoji I) showed signs of uniting with Shivaji but then no concrete result was obtained.

On return to Raigad, Shivaji seized most of Ekoji's possessions in the Mysore plateau. Ekoji's wife Deepabai a scholar of saintly bent of character brought reconciliation between the two brothers so they were not enemies and maintained the status quo of co-existing independent.

## Death and Succession Crisis

Shivaji died on 2 April 1680, on the eve of Hanuman Jayanti. In a span of 50 years he started from a jagir and ended with a vast empire streching from hilly terrains to southern plain.

After Shivaji's unexpected death in April 1680, and his eldest son Sambhaji took power after being challenged by his stepmother Soyarabai.

Meanwhile, Emperor Aurangzeb's son had a falling out with his father and joined forces with Sambhaji, thereafter Aurangzeb personally lead his vast imperial army to attack and completely destroy the Maratha threat once and for all. He threw the full might of the Mughal Empire toward this goal and for a while it seemed that he would achieve his objective.

However, after the capture, torture and the murder of Sambhaji -for his refusal to bow down before Aurangzeb and convert to Islam - turmoil and uncertainty gripped the Marathas who were now on the run and were forced to move their capital from Raigad near Pune to Gingee in the south in current day state of Tamil Nadu.

Thereafter the Maratha forces stabilized and were better organized - began to undertake fast raids on the slow moving Mughal columns. Able generals such as Dhanaji Jadhav and Santaji Ghorpade were able to take the initiative and effectively bogged down the powerful but slow moving Mughal army in to a protracted 27 year war. In the last few years of this war both the Maratha generals delivered severe body blows to the Mughals on the shifting battlefields in Maharashtra.

In 1697 Aurangzeb withdrew from the Deccan for the last time in sickness and thereafter recalled his full army a few years later. After this time the Mughals never again posed a great danger to the Marathas. And within sixty years of Auragzeb's death the Marathas under the Peshwa's leadership soundly defeated the Mughals and forced them to sign the Ahmediya treaty whereby they relinquished their vast empire in the sub-continent to the Marathas. They were allowed to keep nominal control of Delhi while the Marathas were able to collect taxes from vast swaths of present day India and Pakistan, and down all the way to the Southern tip of the subcontinent.

## Rule and Administration

*Fig.: Shivaji statue at Pratapgad*

Shivaji was an able administrator who established a government that included modern concepts such as cabinet (*Ashtapradhan mandal*), foreign affairs (*Dabir*) and internal intelligence. Shivaji established an effective civil and military administration. He also built a powerful navy. Maynak Bhandari was one of the first chiefs of the Maratha Navy under Shivaji, and helped in both building the Maratha Navy and safeguarding the coastline of the emerging Maratha Empire. He built new forts like Sindhudurg and strengthened old ones like Vijaydurg on the west coast. The Maratha navy held its own against the British, Portuguese and Dutch.

Shivaji is well known for his benevolent attitude towards his subjects. He believed that there was a close bond between the state and the citizens. He encouraged all accomplished and competent individuals to participate in the ongoing political/military struggle. He is remembered as a just and welfare-minded king. He brought revolutionary changes in military organisation, fort architecture, society and politics.

Shivaji was the first king of the medieval world to undertake the revolutionary idea of abolishing the feudal system, 150 years before its worldwide recognition in the French revolution. For a span of about 50 years, there were no feudals in his kingdom. After the fall of Raigad in 1689, Raja Ram started giving land grants to Maratha chieftans to fight against the Mughals in the War of 27 years.

❑❑❑

# Chapter 3

# Early Life of Shivaji

The childhood of Shivaji, the founder of the Maratha Empire in the Indian subcontinent, is a topic of great interest in the popular culture of India, espescially in Maharashtra. The earliest detailed descriptions of Shivaji's birth and boyhood are found in the works composed 150 years after his death.

By this time, Shivaji had become a semi-legendary figure, and several stories had developed around his legend. Historian Jadunath Sarkar notes: "The stories told in the later Marathi bakhars about the history of his parents during the year preceding his birth and the events of his own life up to the age of twenty, are in many points contrary to authentic history, and in others improbable, or, at all events, unsupported by any evidence."

## Birth

Shivaji was born in the hill-fort of Shivneri near the city of Junnar. While Jijabai was pregnant, she had prayed the local deity (devi) called "Shivai" for the good of her expected child. Shivaji was named after this local deity.

## Birth Date

The exact birthdate of Shivaji has been a matter of dispute among the historians. The Government of Maharashtra accepts the 3rd day of the dark half of Phalguna, 1551 of Saka calendar (Friday, 19 February 1630) as the official birthdate of Shivaji. This date is supported by several other historians including Dr. Bal Krishna. A horoscope of Shivaji found in the possession of Pandit Mithalal Vyas of Jodhpur also supports this birthdate. According to Setu Madhavrao Pagdi, Shivaji's court poet Paramanand has also mentioned Shivaji's birth date as 19 February 1630.

However, some some other historians such as Jadunath Sarkar and Rao Bahadur Sardesai believed that Shivaji was born in 1627. The various suggested dates include:

- the second day of the light half of Vaisakha in the year 1549 of Saka calendar i.e. Thursday, 6 April 1627.
- 10 April 1627
- May 1627

Sarkar believed that there are no contemporary reliable records of Shivaji's exact birth date and boyhood, and the *bakhars* composed years after his birth contain several unreliable anecdotes. Dr. Bal Krishna rejects teh date suggested by Sarkar, criticizing him for over dependence on 91-Qalmi Bakhar (composed in 1760s) and Shivadigvijaya Bakhar (composed in 1818).

## Parents

Shivaji's father Shahaji Bhonsle was the leader of a band of mercenaries that serviced the Deccan Sultanates.

His mother was Jijabai, the daughter of Lakhujirao Jadhav of Sindkhed.

[Shahaji Raje Bhosle was an early exponent of guerilla warfare. He was the eldest son of Maloji Bhosale ofVerul (present-day Ellora, Maharashtra). He brought the house of Bhosle into prominence. The princely states of Tanjore, Kolhapur andSatara are Bhosle legacies. He was father of Shivaji, the founder of the Maratha Empire.

Islamic ruler Ibrahim Adil Shah of Bijapur, appointed Hindus to key positions and changed the official court language from Persian toMarathi. Maloji was childless for a long time. Two sons were born to him after seeking blessings from a famous Sufi pir of the time, named Hazrat Shah Sharifji. In honour of the pir, Maloji named his sons Shahaji and Sharifji. Maloji was a capable soldier and eventually became an independent Jagirdar in the court of Adil Shah.

Maharaja Shahaji was an extremely ambitious and capable general. At a young age, Maharaja Shahaji had achieved a lot. He was well known not only for his military and leadership skills but also as a Man who kept his word. Maharaja Shahaji had not lost a single battle in his entire life which made him the prominent Maratha legend who was treated even at par with Nizam and Adilshah.

Maharaja Shahaji had defeated quite a number of eminent commanders of Mughals, Adilshah and Nizamshah. Maharaja Shahaji was prominent in the whole of Hindustan (India) for he had not lost a single battle in his lifetime and had always prevailed no matter what the circumstances. Mughal, Adil, Nizam Sultanates were leaving no stone unturned to get Maharaja Shahaji on their side. When Maharaja Shahaji was serving in the

Adilshahi court, he was awarded the title of Farzand (someone placed much higher than a chief commanding an army of 10,000) which was equivalent to the designation of a Prince. Thus, Maharaja Shahaji was highly revered in the Adilshahi court.

The battle of Bhataudi was fought in 1624 in Ahmednagar, Maharashtra between forces of Maharaja Shahaji, Nizam and the combined forces of Mughalshahi and Adilshahi Sultanates. Shah Jahan had ordered his commander-in-chief Lashkar Khan to finish off Nizamshahi. Accordingly, Lashkar Khan with an army of 120,000 (1.2 lakhs) marched onAhmednagar. The Adilshahi Sultanate had also agreed to help the Mughals.

Adilshahi army amounted to no less than 80,000 Men. Thus, a massive army of 200,000 (2 lakhs) walked on Ahmednagar. On the other hand, Maharaja Shahaji had an army of 20,000 at his disposal. Maharaja Shahaji had assigned 10,000 of these, the task of protecting and defending the Ahmednagar fort and town. The remaining 10,000 were with Maharaja Shahaji.

Such a huge army required huge amount of food and water. Thus, both Mughal and Adil forces were encamped on the bank of the Mehkari River. It flowed North-South. The river had a dam to conserve water, as Ahmednagar experienced water shortage. However, during this period, there had been good amount of rainfall. The river had abundant water and was filled to the brim. Maharaja Shahaji came up with a brilliant idea.

With utmost care, cracks were developed in the dam. It was the time of night; the whole Mughal and Adil encampment was fast asleep. Suddenly, water started gushing out of the dam from each of the cracks. Mughals and Adils were clueless about what was happening. It was, as if a huge wall of irate water was running over the Mughals and Adils.

Everyone started running helter-skelter to save their lives. There was chaos and confusion. The whole encampment was flooded with water. Clothes, rations, arms, ammunitions, cannons and cattle everything drowned. Dead elephants were seen floating in the water. Many were taken as prisoners. As many as 25 renowned, Mughal and Adil chiefs were imprisoned by Maharaja Shahaji. It was a huge win for Maharaja Shahaji, after which Maharaja Shahaji became well known.

At various points of time Maharaj Shahaji allied himself with the Adilshah of Bijapur, the Nizamshah of Ahmednagar and the Mughals. His ultimate ambition was to set up an independent Maratha kingdom. He tried on two occasions, first one after the brutal murder of his father-in-law Lakhuji Rao Jadhav (father of Jijabai) and second in 1636. The second attempt was a formidable challenge.

In the meantime, Jahan Khan, the wazir of Nizam killed Nizam on the reasoning that the Nizam was an incapable and unwise ruler, who couldn't take appropriate decisions and was easily deceived by some people. Jahan Khan greeted Maharaja Shahaji with open hands and asked Maharaja Shahaji to join him.

Maharaja Shahaji started leading Nizam's forces. However, at that time, the Mughal forces on the order of Shah Jahan had slain all the men in relation to Nizam and also killed two pregnant women. This was done to finish off the Nizamshahi, as there wouldn't be any Male heir to the throne of the Nizam. However, Maharaja Shahaji, in order to protect Nizamshahi decided to crown a child named Murtuza, who was in relation with Nizam, as the next Nizam. Maharaja Shahaji assured Murtuza's mother that he would not be harmed and vouched for his safety.

Shahajahan dispatched a force of 48,000 to reduce Maharaji Shahaji, Nizam and his ally Adilshah. Under such mounting attack Adilshah sued for peace. With the withdrawal of Adilshah's support, Maharaja Shahaji could not hold much against the Mughals. His possessions were reduced quickly. In the fort of Mahuli he was besieged. Portuguese did not offer any help from naval side due to fear of the Mughals.

In this war, Maharaja Shahaji fought till the last. But, unfortunately Nizam Murtaza, the little kid, was being kidnapped by Mughals and for the purpose of saving the life of Nizam, it became necessary for Maharaja Shahaji to make compromise. This compromise finished Nizamshahi. Maharaja Shahaji, on the condition of protecting the life of little Mourtaza Nizam at any condition, handed him over to Shahajahan. Nizam was taken away by Shah Jahan to Delhi. He was inducted into Adilshahi.

As a precaution Shahajahan ensured that Shahaji was posted in deep south so as not to pose any challenge to Mughals. He finally became one of the top generals in the Adilshah's army, accepting a Jagir in his court, being based in Bangalur (Present day Bangalore in Karnataka). This is one phase of Shahaji's life.

In 1638, a large Bijapur army led by Ranadulla Khan and accompanied by Shahaji defeated Kempe Gowda III and Bangalore was given to Shahaji as a jagir. Shahaji successfully led the Bijapur army to many victories against the Rajas of southern India. Instead of punishing or executing them, Shahaji reprieved all the Rajas. The Rajas thus developed healthy relations with Shahaji and offered military support to Shahaji whenever required.

After this military defeat, his second phase started. He sent his wife Jijabai as Queen Regent, their younger son Shivaji to Pune to manage his jagir of Pune, their elder son Sambhaji and another son Venkoji from his second wife stayed with him at Bangalore. Shivaji and Sambhaji both emerged as accomplished generals. Meanwhile young Shivaji started capturing territory controlled by Adilshah around Pune.

AdilShah, alarmed by the activities of Shivaji in particular, deceitfully captured Shahaji and imprisoned him as he suspected that Shahaji encouraged Shivaji. Two expeditions were sent simultaneously against Shivaji and his elder brother Sambhaji, who defeated Adilshahi forces. Shivaji meanwhile approached Mughal Emperor Shahjahan asking for help against Adilshah. Fearing another Mughal campaign against Bijapur, Adilshah released Shahaji from prison.

However, the elder son Sambhaji was killed during an expedition due to the treacherous role of Afzal Khan. Later Shivaji killed Afzal Khan. Similarly, Shaista Khan had defeated Shahaji in his second attempt. Shivaji in a daring attack severed three of Shaista's fingers and forced him to retreat.

Thus these events proved that Shahaji had taken a sensible decision in keeping Shivaji in the original stronghold of Pune barring which, like Shahaji, Shivaji would have been imprisoned or killed like his elder brother. This period of crisis was overcome by sacrifice and personal bonds of this royal family. Shahaji actively supported Shivaji in his earlier enterprises, like the campaign against Afzal Khan.

Sensing treachery by Afzal khan, Shahaji was waiting near Bijapur with his army of 17,000. He had warned Badi Begum of Adilshah that, if Afzal Khan and his Adilshahi forces killed Shivaji by deceit, then there wouldn't remain even a brick of the Adilshahi kingdom. Shahaji died c. 1665 while on a hunt, after falling off his horse.]

Shivaji was the fifth son born to Jijabai, three of whom had died as infants; Shivaji's elder brother Sambhaji (not to be confused with his son Sambhaji) was the only one to have survived. While Shivaji was accompanied mostly by his mother, Sambhaji lived with his father Shahaji at present day Bangalore.

During the period of Shivaji's birth, the power in Deccan was shared by three Sultanates – Bijapur, Golkonda, Ahmadnagar. Most of the then Marathas forces had pledged their loyalties to one of these Sultanates and were engaged in a continuous game of mutual alliances and aggression. Legend has it that Shivaji's paternal grandfather Maloji Bhosale was insulted by Lakhujirao Jadhav, a sardar in Nizamshahi of Ahmadnagar, who refused to give his daughter Jijabai in marriage to Shahaji.

This inspired Maloji to greater conquests to obtain a higher stature and an important role under Nizamshahi, something that eventually led him to achieving the title of mansabdar (military commander and an imperial administrator). Leveraging this new found recognition and power, he was able to convince Lakhujirao Jadhav to give his daughter in marriage to his son Shahaji.

Shahaji following in the footsteps of his father, began service with the young Nizamshah of Ahmednagar and together with Malik Amber, Nizam's minister, he won back most of the districts for the Nizamshah from the Mughals who had gained it during their attack of 1600. Thereafter, Lakhujirao Jadhav, Shahaji's father-in-law, attacked Shahaji at the Mahuli fort and laid a siege.

Shahaji was accompanied by Jijabai, who was four months pregnant. After seeing no relief coming from Nizam, Shahaji decided to vacate the fort and planned his escape. He sent Jijabai off to the safety of Shivneri fort, which was under his control. It was here at Shivneri that Shivaji was born. In the meanwhile, suspecting his disloyalty, Lakhujirao Jadhav and his three sons were murdered by the Nizamshah in his court when they came to join his forces.

Unsettled by this incident, Shahaji Raje decided to part ways with the Nizamshahi Sultanate and raise the banner of independence and establish an independent kingdom. After this episode Ahmednagar fell to the Mughal emperor Shah Jahan, and shortly thereafter Shahaji responded by attacking the Mughal garrison there and regained control of this region again. In response the Mughals sent a much larger force in 1635 to recover the area back and forced Shahaji to retreat into Mahuli.

The result of this was that Adilshah of Bijapur agreed to pay tribute to the Mughals in return for the authority to rule this region in 1636. Thereafter, Shahaji was inducted by Adilshah of Bijapur and was offered a distant jagir (landholding) at present-day Bangalore, but he was allowed to keep his old land tenures and holdings in Pune. Shahaji thus kept changing his loyalty among

Nizamshah, Adilshah and the Mughals but always kept his jagir at Pune and his small force of men with him.

## Relation with Parents

All historical accounts agree that Shivaji was extremely devoted to his mother Jijabai. His father Shahaji seems to have neglected Jijabai and Shivaji, in favour of his new and younger wife, Tukabai Mohite. Shahaji's fatherly affection and wealth were directed to Vyankoji, his son with Tukabai.

During the 1630s, Shahaji was involved in campaigns against the Deccan Sultanates and the Mughals. In October 1636, he had to cede Shivneri to the Mughals as per a peace treaty. He retained the control of his ancestral jagir of Pune and Supa. This ancestral jagir was formerly held under Nizam Shah, but in 1636, Shahaji entered the service of Adil Shah of Bijapur. According to *Tarikh-i-Shivaji*, Shahaji placed this jagir under Dadoji Konddeo, who had shown good administrative skills as the *kulkarni* (land-steward) of Malthan. He asked Konddeo to bring Jijabai and Shivaji from Shivneri to Pune, and appointed him as their guardian.

Shahaji spent most of his time in Bijapur, close to Tukabai and Vyankoji. Due to Shahaji's neglect, Shivaji grew very close to his mother, Jijabai, and almost adored her like a deity. Jijabai led a deeply religious, almost ascetic, life amidst neglect and isolation. This religious environment had a profound influence on Shivaji.

Shivaji learned much from his father's failed attempts at political independence, his exceptional military capabilities and achievements, his knowledge of Sanskrit, Hindu ethos, patronage of the arts, his war strategies and peacetime diplomacy. Jijabai also instilled in Shivaji a natural love for self-determination and an aversion to external political domination.

## Education

*Fig.: Shivaji receiving the blessings of the Goddess (bazaar art, 1940's)*

Shivaji was trained at Banglore, along with his brother, under the supervision of Shahji, and later on, at Pune, under the supervision of his mother. *Tarikh-i-Shivaji* states that Dadoji Konddeo trained Shivaji personally, and also appointed an excellent teacher for him. In a short time, Shivaji became a skilled fighter and a good horse-rider. The military commanders Kanhoji Jedhe and Baji Pasalkar were appointed to train Shivaji in martial arts. Gomaji Naik Pansambal taught him swordmanship, and later served as his military advisor.

[Dadoji Kondev (also known as *Dadaji Konddeo* and *Dadoji Kondadev*) was a 16th century revenue expert from India, particularly known for his loyalty towards Shahji. He was also a "Subhedar" (Administrative head) of Kondana Fort (now known as Sinhagad), and thus the Pune region. Dadoji Kondev Gochivade was from a Marathi Deshastha Brahmin of the Kulkarni family from the Daund area in Maharashtra. He hailed from Malthan, in the present day Shirur Tahsil in the Pune District.

Dadoji Kondev was in the service of Shahaji Raje Bhonslé, a nobleman and a commander in the Nizamshahi military of Ahmednagar. Shahaji proved himself as a brilliant commander. He was given independent land near the Pune region. Soon Shahaji Raje Bhosale became a prominent warlord of the region. Due to the constant warfare between the three major powers, Mughals (from north, based in Delhi and Agra),Adilshah (in south, based in Bijapur, current Karnataka State), and Nizam, from east, Shahaji had to be constantly engage in diplomatic and political manouvres. He intended to have an independent kingdom, but couldn't defeat the combined might of the Mughal forces and Adilshah. Eventually, after the death of his father-in-law, Jadhavrao, he joined Adilshah and was sent to Bangalore as a commander of Adilshah's army.

Jedhe Shakawali written by Kanhoji Jedhe and his son Baji Jedhe mentions about Dadoji Konddev as:

*"He developed city Shivapur as per order by Shahajiraje in 1636 and Lal Mahal in Pune in next year."*

Dadoji Konddev was an absolutely pious, completely honest and efficient estate manager of Pune Jahagiri, owned by Rajmata Jijau. RAJMATA Jijau was a daughter of Sinkhedkar Royal family. She was a faithful 'Patiwrata' wife of Shahaji Raje Bhosale and loving and dutiful mother of Shivaji Raje. Dadoji Konddev was born in Janefal town, near Sinkhed-Raja, in Buldhana District. Many historians say that Dadoji was born in a Samvedi lad Brahmin family. Janefal is the VERY FIRST town owned by Sindkhedkar Jadhov family. Other towns like Deulgoan-Raja, Kingaon-Raja, Sindkhed-Raja, have been acquired by them by a pact with Moguls of Delhi; hence these towns have "Raja" adjective added to them. After Jadov family left Janefal and started living in Sindkhed-raja, Dadoji worked as their estate manager in Janefal and got reputation as an honest, efficient estate manager. Subsequently, because of the prevalent political situation, Rajmata Jijau had to reside in Pune jahagiri, Sindkhedkar Jadov selected and appointed Dadoji Konddev as an estate manager of this Jahagiri. Dadoji managed this estate with utmost honesty and efficiency. Because of stability and prosperity, brought out by Dadoji's

> management, in this estate, Shivaji Maharaj could
> lay the foundation of an independent maratha
> kingdom.]

Historians have debated whether Shivaji was literate
or not. A few authors, writing centuries after Shivaji's
death, mention that he had mastered several arts and
sciences at a young age.

However, no contemporary records contain any
information about his book-learning. Several letters,
allegedly written by Shivaji or containing lines written by
Shivaji, are available. However, the authenticity of these
letters has not gained universal acceptance among the
historians.

Jadunath Sarkar writes:

*"The weight of evidence is in favour of the view that
Shivaji was unlettered, like three other heroes of medieval
India — Akbar, Haidar Ali, and Ranjit Singh. The
many Europeans who visited him never saw him write
anything; when they presented any petition to him the
Rajah always passed it on to his ministers to be read
to him. No piece of writing in his own hand is known
to exist."*

However, other historians state that *Shivbharat*, written
by Shivaji's court poet Paramanand, indicates that he was
a literate. Shivaji's naming of forts in Sanskrit language
also indicates that he was literate.

Whether or not Shivaji was literate, it is well-known
that he had mastered the two great Hindu epics, Ramayana
and Mahabharata, by listening to recitations and story-
tellings. The noble examples mentioned in the epics greatly
impressed his young mind. He was deeply interested in

religious teachings, and sought the society of Hindu and Muslim saints wherever he went.

## Early Associates

As the administrator of Shahaji's jagir, Dadoji Konddeo established complete control over the Maval region. He won over most of the local Maval *deshpande* (chiefs), and subdued others. Shivaji drew his earliest trusted comrades and a large number of his soldiers from this region. Some of the early Mavlans associated with Shivaji were the chieftains Yesaji Kank and Baji Pasalkar, who were of his own age. Tanaji Malusare, a young deshmukh of Konkan, was another of his early associates.

[Tanaji Malusare, also known as *Simha* (Lion), was a warrior and military leader in the army of Shivaji, founder of theMaratha Empire in 17th century India. Tanaji was one of Shivaji's closest friends hailing from Malusare Clan; the two had known each other since childhood. Tanaji is famously known for the battle of Sinhagad in 1670. At Shivaji's request, he pledged to recapture the fortress of Kondana near Pune. According to many accounts, he received the summons at his son's wedding, and immediately left the festivities. Tanaji Malusare and his troops scaled the fort with the help of mountain lizards (ghorpad in Marathi). He and his men valiantly recaptured the fort from Udaybhan Rathod, fortkeeper of Jai Singh I.

A fierce combat took place between Tanaji and Udaybhan. Udaybhan managed to rid Tanaji of his shield, still Tanaji fought Udaybhan by tying a cloth over one of his hands and using it to ward off Uday Bhan's sword attacks. Tanaji managed to fight Uday Bhan for some time. However, Tanaji lost his life in the battle, and Shivaji renamed the fort from Kondana to Sinhagad in his honor. His words after hearing about the demise of Tanaji were "Gad ala pan Sinha gela"(Meaning although the fort was captured a lion was lost in the battle) However some historical texts account that the name Sinhagad existed long before this incident.]

In the company of his Maval comrades, a young Shivaji wandered over the hills and forests of the Sahyadri range, hardening himself and getting a first-hand knowledge of the land. By 1639, he was surrounded by able and loyal officers. Around 1639, his father had sent four officers:

- Shamrao (or Shyamraj) Nilkanth Ranjhekar (or Rozefyar), the Peshwa (Prime Minister/Chancellor).

- Balkrishna Hanumante, the Muzumdar/ Majumdar (Accountant-General)

- Sonaji Pant or Sonopant, the dabir (secretary)

- Raghunath Ballal Korde, sabnis (paymaster)

In addition to these, Shivaji appointed two more important officers on his own:

- Tukoji Chor Maratha, the sar-i-naubat (commander-in-chief)

- Narayan Pant, the divisional paymaster

## Foundations of Self-rule

In 1644, Shahaji had Lal Mahal built in Pune for his wife and his son Shivaji. A royal seal in Sanskrit which read, *"This is the royal seal of Shivaji, son of Shahaji. This royal seal is for the welfare of people. This seal (the rule of the seal) will grow like the new moon grows"*, was handed to Shivaji. Thus Shivaji started his career as an independent young prince of a small kingdom on a mission. However, Shivaji used the title of *Raja* (king) only after Shahaji's death.

[The *Lal Mahal* (Red Palace) of Pune is one of the most famous monuments located in Pune, India. In the year 1630 AD, Shivaji's Father Shahaji Bhonsle, established the Lal Mahal for his wife Jijabai and son. Shivaji stayed here for several years until he captured his first fort. The original Lal Mahal fell into ruins and the current Lal Mahal is a reconstruction of the original and located in the center of the Pune city.

Shivaji's marriage with his first wife, Saibai took place in Lal Mahal. The original Lal Mahal was built with the idea of rejuvenating the recently razed city of Pune when Dadoji Kondev entered the city along with Shivaji and his mother, Jijabai. Shivaji grew up here, and stayed in the Lal Mahal till he captured the Torna fort in 1645. Towards the end of the 17th Century, the Lal Mahal fell into ruins and was eventually razed to the ground as a result of various attacks on the city. It is said that during the construction of the Shaniwarwada, some soil and stones of the Lal Mahal were used for luck.

In 1734-35, a few houses were constructed on the land of the Lal Mahal and given for use to Ranoji Shinde and Ramchandraji. The records in the offices of the Peshwas mention that Lal Mahal was used for arranging feasts for the Brahmins during the thread-ceremony of Sadoba, son of Chimajiappa.

The exact original location of the Lal Mahal is unknown, however it was known to be very close to the location of Shaniwarwada, which is roughly where the current reconstruction stands. The current Lal Mahal was built only on a part of the land of the original Lal Mahal. The new Lal Mahal was not rebuilt in the same fashion as the original one and there is not much information found about the area and structure of the original Lal Mahal. The current Lal Mahal was rebuilt by the PMC. Construction started in 1984 and was completed in 1988.

Historically, the Lal Mahal is famous for an encounter between Shivaji and Shaista Khan where Shivaji cut off the later's fingers when he was trying to escape from the window of the Lal Mahal. This was part of a surreptitious guerrilla attack on the massive and entrenched Mughal Army that had camped in Pune, with Shaiste occupying (possibly symbolically) Shivaji's childhood home. As a punishment for the ignomy of the defeat despite superior numbers and better armed and fed soldiers, Shaiste was transferred by the Mughal Emperor to Bengal. Even today, Shaiste Khan is regarded as a national hero in Bangladesh- the Muslim homeland of Bengalis. Monuments to him stand testimony to it in Dhaka, capital of modern Bangladesh. The current Lal Mahal is a memorial holding a collection of large size oil-paintings based on the significant events in the life of Shivaji, a statue of Rajmata Jijabai, a carving depicting Shivaji using a gold plough along with Dadoji Konddeo and Jijabai, a fiber model of Raigad with horsemen and a huge map of Maharashtra indicating the forts of Shivaji. The popular Jijamata Garden is now a recreational park for kids.]

## Earliest Conquests

The Chitnis Bakhar (1810), described by later authors as of questionable accuracy, mentions that Shivaji defeated and killed Krishnaji Nayak Bandal, the deshmukh of Hirdas Maval, who had refused to accept Dadoji Konddeo's orders. However, Jadunath Sarkar believes this to be incorrect, and states that this subjugation was completed by Dadoji Konddeo himself. Shivaji along with his Mavala friends and soldiers took an oath to fight for the Swarajya (self-governance) at Rohideshwara temple.

□□□

# Chapter 4

# Shivaji and The Politics of History

Shivaji Bhonsle, venerated in Maharashtra as the father of "the Maratha nation", was born in 1627 into a family of Maratha bureaucrats. His father, Shahji, was the jagirdar of the Sultan of Ahmadnagar in Pune, but he shifted his allegiance to the Sultan of Bijapur; Shivaji's mother, Jiji Bai, was devoted to her son, particularly after her husband took a second wife. This was not the only time that Shahji shifted his loyalties: when the Mughal emperor Shah Jahan decided to lead his forces into the Deccan, Shahji decided to accept the offer of a mansabdari from Shah Jahan.

However, upon the emperor's retreat in 1632, Shahji decided to accept once again the suzerainty of the Sultan of Ahmadnagar. However, the Sultan of Ahmadnagar was taken captive by the Mughal army in 1633, and though Shahji struggled valiantly to retain his political independence, he succumbed to the combined forces of the Mughal Emperor and the Sultan of Bijapur who had signed an accord between themselves in 1636. Shahji surrendered, was expelled from Pune, and retreated to Bijapur.

Shivaji, though his father was exiled from Pune, was raised in the city that was to become the capital not only of Maratha power, but the seat, as it were, of real and imagined Hindu martial traditions. (Much later, it is in Pune that armed resistance to the British led to a campaign of terror and assassination, and it is from Pune that Nathuram Godse, the assassin of Mahatma Gandhi, emerged to press forth the case for a masculine Indian nation-state.) Some historians have argued that Shivaji grew up with a hatred for Islam, but there is little in the historical record that directly substantiates any such reading.

For a good many years, Shivaji and his band of Marathas, who can with some justice be claimed as having originated the idea of guerrilla warfare in India, plundered the countryside, and Shivaji came to acquire a formidable reputation as a warrior. But Shivaji's main interest lay in subduing Bijapur, and the opportunity presented itself when the Sultan, Muhammad Adil Shah, died in November 1656. Muhammad Adil Shah's successor, Ali Adil Shah, sent his general, Afzal Khan, at the head of an army of 10,000 troops to surround and subdue Shivaji in his fortress, Pratapgarh.

The most celebrated act of Shivaji's life, if historians are to be believed, is his killing of Afzal Khan in 1659. According to the most commonly accepted narrative of events, Afzal Khan agreed to meet Shivaji in person to accept his surrender. It is suggested that Afzal Khan had treacherous designs upon Shivaji, but evidently he received a fatal dose of his own medicine before he could murder Shivaji.

The Maratha leader carried a small dagger in one hand, and a tiger's claw in the other, but these little weapons were concealed by the long sleeves of the loose-fitting clothes he wore. As the two men hugged each other, Afzal Khan nearly stuck a dagger at Shivaji's side, but the Maratha passed his arm around the Khan's waist and, to quote from the admiring biography by the Bengali historian Jadunath Sarkar, "tore his bowels open with a blow of steel claws".

It is a chilling fact that this episode, in which neither Afzal Khan nor Shivaji appear to have shown much honor, should have been described, amidst the euphoria of the celebrations in 1974-75 to mark the 300th anniversary of the coronation of Shivaji, as the "most glorious event in the history of the Marathas."

As is purported to be quite common with 'Oriental armies', Afzal Khan's entire force is described as having become panic-stricken at the death of their commander, and Shivaji was left victorious. His triumph over Afzal Khan is often said to mark the birth of Maratha power. In 1664, Shivaji dared even to plunder Surat, a trading town with rich mercantile traditions and immensely wealthy merchants, but this invoked the fury of Aurangzeb, who sent his general Jai Singh to deal with this irritant.

The Mughal commander Jai Singh used a variety of diplomatic and military measures to ease the path to his victory. It is said that Shivaji was visited in his dreams by the goddess Bhavani, who reportedly advised him that he could not triumph if he raised his hand against another Hindu prince, but this reading may be no more than an attempt to assuage the pride of the admirers of Shivaji bothered by Shivaji's capitulation to Aurangzeb.

Though Shivaji himself was incorporated into the Mughal system, becoming in John Richards' words a "vassal" of the Emperor, it was his son, Shambhaji, who was rendered into a mansabdar of 5,000.

Shivaji' hagiographers at this point pause to reflect on their hero's daring escape from the court of Aurangzeb in 1666. Though Shivaji had, by 1670, recaptured many of the fortresses he had previously surrendered to Aurangzeb, the hagiographers do not always mention the fact that he continued to petition the Mughal emperor to be entitled a "Raja". This petition was granted in 1668.

Shivaji's coronation in 1674 as Chhatrapati, or "Lord of the Universe", constitutes the next pivotal chapter in his biography. It was in part to mark his independence from the Mughals, and to repudiate his formal relation to them of a feudatory, that Shivaji had himself crowned, but the very gesture of defiance points to the fact that he recognized the overwhelming power of the Mughals. Moreover, as a Shudra or low-caste person, Shivaji had perforce to enact some ceremony by means of which he could be raised to the status of a Kshatriya or traditional ruler.

To this end, he enlisted the services of Gagga Bhatta, a famous Brahmin from Benares, who did the Brahminical thing in falsely certifying that Shivaji's ancestors were kshatriyas descended from the solar dynasty of Mewar. 11,000 Brahmins are reported to have chanted the Vedas, and another 50,000 men are said to have been present at the investiture ceremony, which concluded with chants of, "Shivaji Maharaj-ki-jai!"

The greater majority of the historians of previous generations and other scholars who have written on Shivaji have supposed that his battles with Aurangzeb, as well as his coronation, cannot be read as other than clear signs of his unrelenting hatred for Muslims and his desire to be considered a great Hindu monarch. But it is not at all transparent, as some recent work suggests, that his conflicts with Aurangzeb should be read through the lens of a communalist-minded history, where all conflicts are construed as the inevitable battle between Islam and Hinduism. It is precisely to thwart the communalist interpretations of Shivaji that Nehru made the pointed remark, in his Discovery of India, that "Shivaji, though he fought Aurangzeb, freely employed Muslims".

The first Pathan unit joined Shivaji's forces in 1658, and one of his trusted commanders who was present at Shivaji's encounter with Afzal Khan was a Muslim, Didi Ibrahim. There is nothing to suggest that the animosity between the Shia rulers of Bijapur and the Sunni Mughal Emperors was of a different order than the conflict between the Hindu Shivaji and Aurangzeb, who were locked in battle over political power and economic resources.

It is also a telling fact that, after the coronation, Shivaji struck a military alliance with the Muslim leader Abul Hasan, the Qutb Shah Sultan, and together they waged a campaign against Shivaji's own half-brother, Vyankoji Bhonsle. Shivaji died in 1680. In recent years, with the advent to power of the Bharatiya Janata Party in national politics, and of the Shiv Sena in Maharashtra, the stock of Shivaji Bhonsle (1627-1680), the Maratha leader, has once again risen high. One hundred years ago, the Indian nationalist Bal Gangadhar Tilak succeeded to a considerable extent in reviving the political memory of Shivaji, and early nationalists, in search of martial heroes, raised him to the eminence of a "freedom fighter".

Tilak's contemporary, the Indian nationalist Lala Lajpat Rai, nicknamed the "Lion of the Punjab", published a biography of Shivaji in Urdu (1896), and commended him to the attention of the youth with the observation that "Shivaji protected his own religion, saved the cow and the Brahmin but he did not disrespect any other religion. This is the highest praise that can be bestowed on a Hindu hero like Shivaji in the days of Aurangzeb."

Shivaji has assumed over the course of the last few years an extraordinary importance in the debates over the Indian past. To visit Maharashtra, particularly Pune, is to come to the awareness that a great many public institutions and buildings have been named after him.

Victoria Terminus in Bombay, one of the preeminent landmarks of European colonialism in what was Britain's foremost colony, is now Chhatrapati Shivaji Terminus, and one would imagine that Maharashtra, home to great saints, writers, and such nationalist leaders as the scholar Gopal Krishna Gokhale, was bereft of any other commanding personality.

Even in Delhi the gigantic Interstate Bus Terminal (ISBT), which services the needs of millions of people every year, has recently been renamed the Chhatrapati Shivaji Bus Terminal. It is presumed that Shivaji was one of the earliest exponents of the idea of a Hindu nation, who kept the torch of Hindu resistance alive during the days of Muslim rule (generally characterized as 'Muslim tyranny'). Lala Lajpat Rai, whom we have quoted previously, took the view that Shivaji's life demonstrated that "during any [sic] time in Muslim rule Hindus did not lose any opportunity to show their valour and attain freedom nor did they quietly suffer oppression."

So long as Indian nationalists persisted in portraying Shivaji as a Hindu leader who withstood Aurangzeb's military campaigns and religious fanaticism, they were given no hindrance by the British; but when Tilak invoked Shivaji's name and courage to rouse Indians to resistance against British rule, he was convicted of sedition.

The emergence of Gandhi, and the adoption by the Indian National Congress of non-violence as its official policy, did little to erode the popularity in which Shivaji was held.

His name was kept alive by armed revolutionaries and by a nation, stung by charges that it was effete and incapable of offering resistance, eager to flaunt a martial past; and the emergence of communalism in the 1920s, leading eventually to demands for the creation of a Muslim state, again made it possible to urge resistance to Muslim demands in the name of Shivaji.

With the creation in 1960 of the new state of Maharashtra, carved out of the old Bombay Presidency, Shivaji became canonized as the creator of the Marathi nation, and the celebration in 1974 of the 300th anniversary of his coronation was to furnish ripe opportunities for consolidating the view that he was even a 'national' leader. To take any other view was to invite retribution, as one Marathi historian at Marathwada University found out in 1974 when he was dismissed from his position for disputing the hagiographic view of Shivaji.

One volume of contributions, mainly by historians, was entitled Chhatrapati Shivaji: Architect of Freedom (1975). Its editor states that Shivaji "laid the foundation of a nation-state, the state of the Marathas, on a firm, secular basis." But what is this nation-state of the Marathas, and of what "freedom" was Shivaji the architect?

Doubtless, the Marathas were the dominant power in the Deccan for much of the eighteenth century, but the argument for Maratha sovereignty, and a Maratha nation-state, cannot so easily be sustained.

Shivaji's successors, taking advantage of the weakness of the later Mughals, would play more the role of plunderers and marauders than kings while still acting as the tax-collectors for the Mughal emperors; by the second half of the eighteenth century, they were also contending with the military strength of the East India Company's forces, though they were nonetheless able to capture Delhi and Agra, the nerve centers of the Mughal empire, in 1770-71.

Similarly, it is only possible to characterize Shivaji as the "architect of freedom" on the presumption that Hindus were laboring under severe disadvantages and were suffocated by Muslim tyranny before Shivaji freed them from their woes. One historian, taking this view, put the matter rather dramatically in another volume commemorating the tercentenary of Shivaji's coronation when he described Shivaji as having liberated the Marathas from three centuries of "alien rule" which had "turned the natives fatalistic": "It was Shivaji who emancipated them from this terrific mental torpidity. He created in them self-confidence . . . He gave them back their dearly loved religious freedom."

Yet this assessment appears almost moderate, when we consider R. C. Majumdar's opinion that in the whole history of India, there was no Hindu other than Shivaji "who made such a pious resolve in his mind to save his country and religion from foreign yoke and oppression."

Dismissing with utter contempt the position of "modern Hindu politicians and pseudo-historians" [a reference to Nehru among others] who insist on "a complete assimilation between the Hindus and Muslims after the first fury of intolerance and oppression was over", Majumdar remarked: "But Shivaji was in any case free from such ideas. He looked upon the Muslims as oppressive rulers and the Hindus as long-suffering subject peoples."

To substantiate the Hindu communalist reading of Shivaji as the architect of Hindu freedom requires that Hindu-Muslim conflict be seen as the backdrop of his own times, just as it turns him into an inveterate foe of Muslims.

Yet Shivaji employed Muslims in his army, among them 700 Pathans who had once worked for the Bijapur Sultan, and he forged alliances with Muslim rulers, in one case to wage a campaign against his own half-brother.

It is not at all clear why the conflict between Shivaji and Aurangzeb should necessarily be viewed as a Hindu-Muslim conflict, rather than as a contest over power, resources, and sovereignty.

Moreover, there is little documentary evidence to warrant the conclusion that Hindus in the Deccan were being systematically persecuted before Shivaji arrived to free them from their yoke. Indeed, quite to the contrary, at least some of the evidence points to the fact that many

Muslim dynasties in the south (mainly Shiite) retained a catholic attitude towards Hinduism.

Few historians in the 1970s, as communalism was becoming an important force in the writing of Indian history, were prepared to reflect on how far it is possible to infer from Shivaji's encounters with Afzal Khan and Aurangzeb that people belonging to various social strata similarly felt their lives to be bounded by oppositional religious feelings.

Yet, just as Aurangzeb and Akbar had become symbolic figures in the emerging dispute between secularists and communalists, so Shivaji was to become an iconic figure in the struggle to define the 'authentic' history of India.

With the rise to power of the Bharatiya Janata Party at the national level, and earlier of the Shiv Sena in Maharashtra, the quest for a martial Hindu past has received a new impetus, and since the conflict has moved to the domain of history as well, it seems certain that Shivaji will continue to be viewed not merely as a chieftain and even Maratha leader, which he doubtless was, but – altogether erroneously – as the supreme figure in the "Hindu struggle for freedom" from Muslim tyranny and as the inspirational figure for Indian independence.

Shivaji's acolytes, in recent years, have embraced tactics of intimidation and terror that certainly do no credit to Shivaji himself.

The scholar James Laine, author of Shivaji: Hindu King in Islamic India, was placed under a death sentence for the expression of views considered detrimental to Shivaji, and Oxford University Press was compelled to withdraw the book from sale in India. One of Professor Laine's local informants, a scholar at the venerable Bhandarkar Oriental Research Institute (BORI), was publicly humiliated by hoodlums claiming to act in the name of venerating Shivaji's memory, and the institute itself was sacked.

Any intellectual history of how Shivaji's name survives in India will thus have to contend not only with such obvious phenomena as the rise of the Shiv Sena, but also the strategies deployed to silence those who question the received versions of the history of Shivaji.

□□□

# Chapter 5

# Shivaji's Forts

Shivaji, the founder of Maratha Empire in Western India in 1664 was well known for his forts; he was in possession of around three hundred at the time of his death. Many, like Panhala Fort and Rajgad existed before him but others like Sindhudurg and Pratapgad were built by him from scratch. Also the fort of Raigad was built as the place of throne, i. e. the capital, of Maratha Empire by Hiroji Indulkar on the orders of Shivaji. This is the holy place where Shivaji was coronated and today also his Samadhi stands in front of the Jagadishwar temple.

These forts were central to his empire and their remains are among the foremost sources of information about his rule. The French missionary Father Fryer witnessed the fortifications of Gingee, Madras, built by Shivaji after its conquest, and appreciated his technical knowhow and knowledge.

[Gingee is a panchayat town in Villupuram district (erstwhile South Arcot district) in the Indian state of Tamil Nadu. The nearest town with a railway station is Tindivanam, 28 km away and Thiruvannamalai, 39 km. Gingee is located between three hills covering a perimeter of 3 km.

Gingee is famous for its Gingee Fort, a popular tourist attraction. The Kon dynasty laid the foundations for the gingee fort in 1190 AD. The Fort in Gingee was later built by the Chola dynasty in 13th century. In 1638, Gingee came under the control of Bijapur Sultanate from Vijayanagar. In 1677, it was under the control of Maratha king Shivaji. In 1690, it changed to be under Mughal, under whose rule it became the headquarters of Arcot. It changed hands to the French in 1750, and then to the British in 1762. In the 18th century, it was occupied again by the French for 11 years. During this time, many sculptural aspects of Gingee were shifted to Pondicherry by the French. To visit Gingee fort, guides are available from archaeological office which is on the way to the fort. The office is open for visitors from 9:00 to 17:00.

The founding of the Kon dynasty provides the launching of Gingee as a fortified royal center . The Gingee country then came under the rule of the Hoysalas in the later part of the 13th and in the first half of the 14th century. From the Hoysalas it passed on, by relatively easy efforts, into the hands of the first rulers of Vijayanagara empire. The Vijayanagar dominion gradually expanded over South India and divided the administration into three important provinces, which were under the control of Nayaks.

These were the Nayaks of Madurai, Nayaks of Tanjore and Nayaks of Gingee. Information about the Gingee Nayaks and their rule is very scanty. It is said that Tupakula Krishnappa Nayaka (1490 to 1521) of a Chandragiri family was the founder of the Nayaka line of Gingee kings. He seems to have ruled gloriously all over the coast from Nellore down to the Coleroon up to 1521 AD. Under the Nayaks the Forts were strengthened and the town was greatly enlarged.

The last Nayak of Gingee was forced to surrender to the Bijapur army towards the end of December 1649 AD. The booty acquired by the Mohammedan rulers of Bijapur was 20 crores of rupees in cash and jewels. Gingee assumed a new and enhanced strategic importance under the Bijapur governors. Bijapur was in possession of the fortress of Gingee till 1677 AD, when the famous Chatrapati Shivaji, the son of Shahaji fell upon it in his momentous Carnatic expedition. The Marathas greatly strengthened and fortified its defences.

The Mughals were then able to capture the fort of Gingee in the Carnatic from Rajaram the King of the Marathas, early in 1698, after a protracted and weak siege of seven years. Zulfikar Khan, the son of Asad Khan, the Grand Vizir in the court of Aurangazeb, was in command of the siege operation of Gingee and of its governor till he left the Carnatic after about a year from its fall.

After that Aurangazeb, granted a mansab of 2,500 rank and jagir of 12 lakhs to Swarup Singh, a Bundela Chieftain, along with the killedari of Gingee in 1700 AD. Raja Sawrup Singh died of old age in 1714 AD. His arrears of payments due to the faujdari amounted to 70 lakhs, being a defaulter for ten years. The Nawab of Arcot reported this matter to the Badshah (Mughal Emperor) at Delhi.

Hearing about the death of his father, Desingh, the son of Raja Sarup Singh, started for Gingee from Bundelkhand, his ancestral home.

On arriving at Gingee, Desingh assumed the government of Gingee after performing the last rites of his father. Aurangazeb had granted a firman to his father and Desingh took formal possession of his father's jaghir on ground of his hereditary right. Desingh did not receive a warm welcome from the Mughal officers. The Nawab of Arcot, Sadatullah Khan, who attempted to dispossess Desingh, pleaded that the firman was not valid. When Payya Ramakrishna, who was his secretary, informed him of the legal necessity of getting the firman renewed by the new Emperor before assuming the jaghir, Desingh replied that he had got the firman of Aurangazeb and that he need not apply to anybody else.

In fact after regaining the fort from Marathas, Aurangzeb had first appointed Nawab Daud Khan as the deputy subhadar of the Deccan. Nawab Daud Khan removed his headquarters from Gingee to the town of Arcot, as he believed that the place was not healthy. This diminished the importance of Gingee. While shifting his headquarters, Daud Khan appointed Sadatullah Khan as his Diwan and Faujdar in 1708. Sadatullah Khan later became the Nawab of the two Carnatics in 1713, under Nizam-Ul-Mulk. He was the regular and acknowledged Nawab of the Carnatic between the years 1710 and 1732 AD. After the death of Raja Swarup Singh he renewed the demand for the arrears of revenue with his son Raja De Singh.

This led to a battle between the two, which unfortunately ended in the death of the young and valiant Rajput, Desingh on 3 October 1714.

The gallantry displayed by Desingh at the young age of 22, against the powerful Nawab Sadatulla Khan of Arcot in a struggle that was hopeless from the outset (Desingh's army consisted of only 350 horses and 500 troopers, while the Nawab's army had 8,000 horsemen and 10,000 sepoys) has made us remember him forever. The ballets are sung in and around Gingee till date about his bravery. However, the fortress of Gingee lost its pre-eminent position and political importance within a few years of the extinction of the Rajput rule.

Subsequently, the two European rival powers in India, the English and the French, got themselves involved in the internal quarrels and fights and the French won for themselves the Gingee fortress on the 11th Sept., 1750, under the initiative of Bussy. They took good care to secure the fort by a strong garrison, which was well supported with artillery and ammunition.

Gingee remained firmly in French possession until after the fall of Pondicherry to Sir Eyre Coote in January 1761. The English commander was Captain Stephen Smith. With the fall of Gingee the French lost their last possession in the Carnatic.

Gingee regained its political importance, for the last time in its fateful history, in 1780 AD, when Haidar Ali, helped by some able French Officers, invaded Carnatic with a force of 90,000 men.

Haidar's men appeared before the fortress and easily carried it by their assault in November 1780. The English re-conquered it at the close of the second Mysore war from Tippu Sultan in 1799. After that Gingee had been free from the ravages and anarchy of war, but subject to desolation and decay. During the frequent Indo-French Wars, the British resident wanted the Fort and The Fortification to be demolished. Luckily his suggestion was not accepted and the Fort remains for us to experience and relive the history. The presence of Muslim rulers in Gingee is evident from the inhabitants of a near by village called Minambur, where the urdu speaking Navaitha Muslims living with their unique culture and tribes such as Shakir, Koken, Bhanday Bhonday, Choudary, Pappa, Aghalay, Hazari, Amberkhani, etc.]

Sindhudurg was built in order to control the attacks of Portuguese and Siddhis on coastal areas of Maratha Empire. This fort is the witness of Shivaji's Navy which was later led by Kanhoji Angre in times of Shivaji's grandson Shahu I, and came to glory. Also Shivaji built the forts of Colaba and Underi to control the activities of the Siddhis in Arabian Sea. At the time of Underi's construction British opposed a lot and stood with their warships in the sea to obstacle the material being supplied for the construction of the fort. But for their surprise the material required for construction was being supplied with the help of small boats in night.

The hill fort Salher in Nashik district was at a distance of 1200 km from the hill fort Jingi, near Chennai. Over such long distance, hill forts were supported by seaforts.

The seafort, Kolaba Fort, near Mumbai was at a distance of 500 km from seafort Sindhudurg. These all forts were put under a havaldar with a strong garrison. Strict discipline was followed. These forts proved useful during Mughal-Maratha wars.

Along with Rana Kumbha of Mewar and Raja Bhoj of Shilahar, he stands as a grand figure in the art of fortification in Indian sub-continent. There are a number of legends about these forts. Even today thousands of youths visit these forts in his memory.

Notable features of Shivaji's forts include:

- Design changes with the topography and in harmony of the contour, no monotony of design
- No ornate palaces or dance floors or gardens
- No temple complexes
- Not much difference in the area of higher or lower ranks
- Marvelous acoustics in the capital
- Sanskritization of fort names
- Community participation in the defense of forts
- Three tier administration of forts
- System of inspection of forts by higher ups including the king
- Distinct feature of forts like double line fortification of Pratapgad, citadel of Rajgad
- Foresight in selection of sites.

□□□

# Chapter 6

# Coronation of Shivaji Maharaj

## The Saffron Morning of the Rising Sun of Hindavi Swarajya

On the 13th day (trayodashi) of the first fortnight of the month of 'Jyeshtha' as per the Hindu calendar, in the year 1596, the coronation ceremony was held to enthrone Punyashlok Chhatrapati Shivaji Maharaj as the King of Hindavi Swaraj. The grand function took place atop the 5,000-ft high Raigad fort in Maharashtra. He became thereafter a full-fledged Chhatrapati - a Hindu emperor in his own right. The occasion holds up for the Hindu people inspiring lessons for their future march - perhaps unequalled by any other single event during the past 3-4 centuries of their history. It is the golden day of glory in the history of Hindusthan and Hindus.

When Hindustan was burning under barbaric attacks by the Mughals and when Hindus were loyally serving the Muslims Adilshahs and Badshahs all over India, there was oppression of women, cows, language and temples. The Sultans had converted the whole country into a slaughterhouse. Hindu society was going towards annihilation under Muslim assaults and the blazing Sun of independence had set.

In such adverse conditions, exhibiting great bravery, valour and sacrifice, Chhatrapati Shivaji Maharaj established the independent sovereign Hindavi Swaraj by defeating Mughal kings and thus protected Hindus, Hindu Dharma and Hindustan. It was these almost superhuman challenges that Shivaji had accepted even as a teenaged boy. He encouraged Hindus to obliterate Muslim attackers.

He created a great future for Hindustan. Thus unto Chhatrapati Shivaji Maharaj, undoubtedly, belongs the chief credit of lighting up the torch of the final freedom struggle against the backdrop of several centuries of Islamic aggression, and ultimately reducing that foreign slavery to ashes. Chhatrapati Shivaji Maharaj created self-confidence amongst Hindus. He made Hindus realize that they had the might of lions but were leading their lives like sheep.

Shivaji Maharaj visited major shrines in Maharashtra before his coronation. He also performed pujas for Mahadeva, Bhavani and other Deities. The ceremony was going on from 30th May to 6th June i.e. for a full week. The crowning was being done with the chanting of holy Veda-mantras and sprinkling holy water from seven rivers and seven seas. People from all castes were allowed to anoint (sprinkle) the king with Panchamrit and holy waters from different places. While anointing him, they used to say.

"You are our crowned king (Chhatrapati Raje), you are our protector. We pray unto you to please look after us like a father." Simultaneously the Ved Mantras were resounding in the hall. As Shivaji mounted the throne for the coronation, the priests chanted the holy verses. Musical instruments began to play and the artillery of all the forts fired salvos of their guns.

The main priest held the royal umbrella and hailed him as Shiva Chhatrapati. He was conferred the title of 'Kshatriya Kulavantas Sinhasanadheeshwar Chhatrapati Shivaji Maharaj' by the priest.

This uprising by the Marathas was to protect the Hindu religion, to toss away the yoke of foreigners and to establish an independent and powerful Hindavi Samrajya (empire). All efforts of Shivaji were overflowing with intense patriotism. People also had become aware of it and hence he was welcomed every where in India, be it the South, North, East or West, as 'the protector of Hindus'. Hindus thought him to be a supporter of their cause.

The contemporary history, legends and literature of that time are full of appreciation and respect for him. There were requests pouring in for Shivaji to rescue Hindus from many towns and states of India.

When the Marathas tore the green flags of Muslims and hoisted saffron flags, no Hindu had dared to get crowned after the fall of the kingdom of Vijayanagar. This crowning ceremony was a blow to the invincibility of Muslims. Shivaji had the feeling that he was not protecting his own kingdom but was striving for the protection of Dharma.

Rightly did the great Hindi bard Bhushana, who forsook the royal favours of the Mughal court to come over to Shivaji to record his glories, sing:

Kashiji ki kalaa jaati, Mathura masjid hoti |

Shivaji na hote to sunnat hoti sab ki | |

(Had not there been Shivaji, Kashi would have lost
its culture,Mathura would have been turned into
a mosque and all would have been circumcised.)

To remind the people of this day, Shivaji started a
Crowning Era-'Rajyabhishek Shaka'. In the fight for
independence and establishing his own kingdom, in every
aspect Shivaji Maharaj did everything possible to promote
Hinduism. His assembly of eight ministers was formed
based on Hindu ideals. One comes across this concept of
eight ministers in the Ramayan and the Mahabharat. King
Dashrath too had eight ministers.

In the Shantiparva of the Mahabharat also it has been
suggested that an exchange of thoughts of eight ministers
is necessary. During the coronation ceremony, Maharaj
changed the Persian names of the ministers to
Sanskrut.During the coronation ceremony, Maharaj
changed the Persian names of the ministers to Sanskrut
as follows–

| *Persian* | *Sanskrut* |
| --- | --- |
| Peshva | Panta Pradhan |
| Majmuadar | Panta Amatya |
| Vakiya | navis Mantri |
| Shuru | navis Panta Sachiv |
| Dabir | Sumant |
| Sar-e- naubat | Senapati |
| Sadra, Muhatsib | Panditrav, Danadhyaksha |
| Kazi-ul- kujat | Nyayadish |

The motto Shivaji inscribed on his coin even at the early stage of his endeavours amply reflects the age-old Hindu ideal pulsating in Shivaji's mind

His seal which read in Sanskrit:

Pratipatchandralekheva vardhishnurvishwavanditaa |

Shaahasoonosshivasyaisha mudraa bhadraaya raajate | |

'This Royal Seal of Shivaji the son of Shahaji, ever increasing in splendour like the moon on the first day of the bright half of the lunar month, shall shed auspicious benevolence and commands the homage of the entire world.' The successors of Shivaji, the Peshwas had carried the Hindu (saffron) flag right up to Kabul and ultimately crippled the Mughal seat of power, which had remained unchallenged for several centuries never to rise again. They had rightly grasped the life mission of Chhatrapati Shivaji.

Swami Vivekananda once remarked in these glowing terms: "Shivaji is one of the greatest national saviours who emancipated our society and our Dharma when they were faced with the threat of total destruction. He was a peerless hero, a pious and God-fearing king and verily a manifestation of all the virtues of a born leader of men described in our ancient scriptures. He also embodied the deathless spirit of our land and stood as the light of hope for our future."

Thus the celebration of the coronation day of Chhatrapati Shivaji Maharaj carries the spirit of victorious resistance against foreign aggression and presents a glorious vision of national freedom rich with its Hindu content. In today's unstable and perilous times, to get inspiration to win over such a situation, it is necessary for all patriots to celebrate this day with great gusto.

HJS's Appeal to all Hindus to celebrate the day of coronation of Chhatrapati Shivaji:

- All should get up early and have a holy bath like Diwali festival; then apply 'kumkum' on the forehead
- Perform 'puja' of the picture of Chhatrapati Shivaji Maharaj, make sweets and offer them as holy sacrament
- Draw 'rangolis' outside houses
- Put on saffron turbans for the whole day.
- Fly saffron flags on houses and erect 'Gudhis' like 'Gudhi Padva'.

*Quote:* People who sing and dance in a procession organised to celebrate the birth anniversary of Shivaji Maharaj will never understand his importance. However the one who puts in efforts like him will be able perceive his greatness and surrender at his feet! - *H.H. Dr. Jayant Athavale*

Chhatrapati Shivaji Maharaj is the principle of effulgence or rather he is the divine inspiration. He is certainly not human. In fact he is a Primal God who took birth in a divine and pure culture.

HJS salutes Shivaji Maharaj on His Birth Anniversary!

NCERT (National Council of Education Research and Training) has made only a 5 lines mention of Shivaji in the std. 7th text book 'Our Past - 2'. However in stark contrast it gives 60 pages to the Mughals who invaded India and made Indians their slaves. HJS protested against this ploy and compelled Goa Govt. to increase the matter on Shivaji Maharaj. Later Goa Govt. added 5 pages in the syllabus.

The biography of Shivaji Maharaj has an answer for any problem faced by a Hindu or Indian politicians; however for this purpose the biography should be read with shrewdness and insight. If read by Hindus with the immoderate vision of Gandhi with respect to non-violence, truth, pleasing Muslims, or through the coloured spectacles of Nehru, who with the concept of 'all religions are equal', meted out inferior treatment to Hindus, then Hindus will not even become aware of when they were circumscribed ! Gandhi, Nehru and their descendants had created terror in the minds of the people about what they would have to suffer if they even uttered the name of Shivaji Maharaj.

In fact Shivaji Maharaj has been totally eliminated from the history text books at the Secondary school level. History on Shivaji Maharaj is taught and finished in the 3rd or 4th standards as if they are fairy tales for children to read and forget. Politicians have ensured that the youth and adults do not get any inspiration from the biography of Shivaji Maharaj simply because it is an ever flowing spring of inspiration for Hindus!

Since childhood Shivaji Maharaj was fully aware that he had to fight the Mughals. In his book 'Chatrapati Shivaji Maharajanche Saptaprakaranatmak Charitra' Malhar Ramrav Chitnis has described the mindset of Prince Shivaji when living with his father Shahajiraje at Vijapur. He pens Prince Shivaji's thoughts as, "We are Hindus. These Yavans (Muslims) are inferior to us. There is none more inferior than them. I am distressed by serving them, eating food served by them, flattering them or even greeting them. It is so wrong to see the ridicule of one's own religion. As we walk down the road we see cows being slaughtered. At that time I feel like beheading the killers and the distress grows even more.

What is the use of living to see a cow being tormented? I am compelled to remain silent because of being reprimanded by my father otherwise I feel like killing the one indulging in cow slaughter.

It is not at all good to be in the company of Muslims. So also it is inappropriate to go to the court (darbar) of the emperor or to visit any wealthy man." As soon as he returned from the Vijapur court he would bathe and change his clothing. It is at this very age that young Prince Shivaji showed his valorous nature by chopping off the hand of a butcher who was dragging a cow for slaughter in another kingdom!

Inspiration endowed by Chatrapati Shivaji is very clear from the above incidents. The biographer has strengthened this further in the following words of Shivaji Maharaj, "We are Hindus. The entire southern region has been invaded by the Muslims and our religion is going downhill. Hence one should not hesitate to sacrifice even one's life to protect religion. By doing so one would add to one's treasure of valorous deeds". Soon thereafter by taking the vow of Raieshvari and conquering the 'Torana' fort Shivaji Maharaj revealed his nature to the world.

Today people are talking of the concept of 'equality of religions' in society. The Congress party is trying to depict him as non-communal and secular. Nowadays some Hindu protagonists are trying to drag Shivaji Maharaj into the camp of secularism by making statements such as 'there were Muslim soldiers in his army'. Really these are pearls of wisdom by these so-called ardent (hypocritical) lovers of Hinduism!

In this context the author of the book 'Marathi Riyasati' and a great historian, Sardessai writes, 'Towards 1649, 500-700 Pathans from Vijapur came to Shivaji Maharaj in search of jobs. Though he did not approve of employing them, he listened to the counsel of Gomaji Naik Pansabal who advised that `these people have come after hearing about your popularity so please does not disappoint them.

If you remain adamant that you will employ only Hindus and that you do not need others then you will not be able to establish a kingdom. So include all eighteen communities of all four varna (classes) of society and allow them to carry out their own duties". So he employed the servitors of Radho Ballal Korde. However the current Hindu protagonists are ignorant about the facts in this context and about how the monarch also ensured that there were spies to keep watch on those Muslim soldiers!

If these 500- 700 soldiers made any attempt to divide the army then as was prevalent in those days he would also not hesitate to punish them (by throwing them over the cliff). It was not like today when a perpetrator of a heinous crime against the Indian Parliament, instead of being hanged, goes scot free simply because he is a Muslim!

In this context a historian researcher Mr. Ninad Bedekar says, 'A new idea that Chatrapati Shivaji Maharaj had 'several' Muslims in his army is being projected. I will quote a few names. You can give me the rest!' When Prince Shivaji came to the Jagirs of Pune, Indore and Supe, of the representatives of Shahajiraje only three were Muslims, namely Siddi Ambar Bagdadi, Jainkhan

Peerzade and Bahalimkhan. Another Muslim associated with Shivaji Maharaj was Nurkhan Beg, the chief of his infantry. But the truth is that later at some juncture all these people were driven off because no mention of their names is made anywhere in the historical annals. After the year 1675 these people were nowhere in the picture.

The British army also employed Indians as soldiers. Afzal Khan who attacked Shivaji Maharaj employed 3000 Maulas in his army, but can we call him secular? Why then is this cord of secularism wound tightly (like an iguana) only around the necks of Hindus? Claiming that Shivaji Maharaj was secular simply because he had a few Muslim soldiers in his army is an indicator of an over liberal intellect.

### Promotion of Sanskrit

In the fight for independence and establishing his own kingdom, in every aspect Shivaji Maharaj did everything possible to promote Hinduism. His assembly of eight ministers was formed based on Hindu ideals. One comes across this concept of eight ministers in the Ramayan and the Mahabharat. King Dashrath too had eight ministers. In the Shantiparva of the Mahabharat also it has been suggested that an exchange of thoughts of eight ministers is necessary.

During the coronation ceremony, Maharaj changed the Persian names of the ministers to Sanskrut as follows:–

Thinking of Sanskrut names to rename various ministers or forts was a hobby of this great king. In September 1665, that is around the time of Dasra before leaving on a journey he named all the forts from his kingdom. Malhar Ramrav Chitnis in the biography of the monarch, 'Chatrapati Shivaji Maharajanche Saptaprakaranatmak

Charitra' has spoken about the forts saying, "At each place after place Maharaj would build a new fort to frighten the enemy. Varugad, Bhushangad, Mahimagad, Vardhangad, Sadashivgad, Macchindragad are some of them". In the book 'Marathyancha Itihas' it is said, "Shivaji Maharaj loved Sanskrut. There are several instances to testify this. He changed the names of forts to Raigad, Vishalgad, Suvarnagad, Vijaydurg, Prachandgad and Pandavgad.""

Lokmanya Tilak was the first to start the celebration of the birth anniversary of Shivaji Maharaj. He was followed by Svantrya Veer Savarkar in 1908 in London. Both these leaders were fully aware of the importance of this biography, but Gandhi and Nehru both kept strict vigilance over this text ever since the independence of India. This is how the fact that a handful of Muslims invaded and destroyed Hindu kingdoms and gained control over the Hindu empire is not known to most Hindus after 1920.

In fact it is because of this misguidance that they accepted the division of India without offering any resistance to it. Non-acceptance of this biography which would have inspired Indians has resulted in the return of Muslim powers in the form of Pakistan and Bangladesh, to overpower Hindus. It is because the incidents of Shivaji Maharaj tearing open Afzal Khan's abdomen and chopping off Sahishtekhan's fingers being kept secret that today we so easily allow a compromise by releasing hard core terrorists in return for release of the kidnapped daughter of an Indian Muslim Minister, Mufti Mohammed.

India's External Affairs Minister flies to the Kandahar desert in a special plane only to release criminals who have butchered Hindus! In Kashmir Bitta Karate who beheaded 16 Hindus is released on parole! In the 13 days after killing Afzal Khan, Shivaji Maharaj conquered 16 forts and in contrast within a year of India becoming independent, our politicians lost 1/3rd of our motherland in Kashmir to enemies! Fearing Shivaji's valour, as long as he was alive, Aurangzeb did not dare to even talk about conquering South India. Yet today the cunning, crafty Musharraf arrives in India to disrupt an Agra conference or dares to hang the Indian tricolour upside down on his personal aircraft.

His subjects being fully aware of the struggle between Righteousness and unrighteousness! Just as Maharaj was fully aware that he had to fight the Mughals so also were his subjects. The situation was such that people were worried as to whether their Maharaj would return alive from the Agra jail. Despite that, the leaders of home rule (svarajya) and the Maulas did not get unnerved and as per the plan of Shivaji Maharaj they protected his kingdom and ruled it in his absence.

The Maulas were prepared to sacrifice even auspicious events in their families and were willing to face the jaws of death. Sinhagad, Pavankhind, Agra,... how many more forts does one need to quote ? In this struggle between Righteousness and unrighteousness many parents lost their sons and several women were widowed. They were all fully aware of why they were fighting the Mughals. Rather than wishing that their husbands stay at home, these women supported them in their mission against the Mughals.

They clearly choose widowhood, rather than wishing their husbands remain passive but safe as this would have only kept their marital status intact superficially as the women folk would have been raped by the Mughal sardars. Compare this noble attitude of theirs to the tantrums thrown by the relatives of victims of the plane hijacked by terrorists to Kandahar. Both the central government and the majority of people of India seem to forget whom they are fighting this battle against. The entire country is testimony to this.

The politicians of today and most of the people are still unaware of why we drove the British out of India. Our revolutionary Indian heroes have not shed blood in vain. If only we were to understand this then we would not have played cricket matches with Pakistan which is all set to wipe out Hindus in Kashmir, the land of Sage Kashyap. We would also not have given refuge to Bangladeshi infiltrators and would have driven off the Chinese ambassadors who have tried to stake a claim on Arunachal Pradesh. All this is a consequence of not being inspired by Chhatrapati Shivaji Maharaj to fight for independence and home rule!

□□□

# Chapter 7

# Shivaji's Campaigns

After his escape from Agra Shivaji needed time and breathing space to repair his forts and consolidate his army and administration. In April 1667 he sent a letter to Aurangzeb offering submission but the Mughal Emperor ignored this as a ruse and ordered a fresh campaign against the Maratha ruler.

*Fig.: Terrain near Aurangabad*

Shivaji then approached Maharaja Jaswant Singh of Jodhpur and through his influence Aurangzeb recognized Shivaji's title of Raja (March 1688) and returned his fort of Chakan—out of the 23 annexed under the Treaty of Purandar.

For the next two years Shivaji lived at peace with the Mughals—his son Sambhaji was posted to the Mughal viceroy's capital in the Deccan, Aurangabad, as a commander of 5000 cavalry. A jagir in Berar was assigned to him for the expenses of this force. The inevitable rupture between the two sides took place in January 1670— Shivaji's men deserted the Mughal service and he began recovering his forts. First Kondana, then Purandar, Kalian-Bhimri, and finally Mahuli by the end of that year.

At this time the Mughal administration in the Deccan was paralysed by tensions between the viceroy Shahzada Muazzam and his general Dilir Khan. The latter accused the prince and Jaswant Singh of being secretly allied with Shivaji and aiding his recent successes in order to wrest the throne from his father Aurangzeb. Dilir Khan escaped to North India with his force, chased by the other two— Aurangzeb then sent Mahabat Khan to take command of operations and keep Jaswant away from Muazzam.

## Shivaji's Lightning Strikes 1670-72 [mh]

Shivaji utilized the Mughal infighting to sack the rich port of Surat in September 1670—he is estimated to have carried off Rs. 66 lakh worth of booty. In later years he demanded the annual payment of *chauth* (quarter of Surat's revenue) explaining, *"As your emperor has forced me to keep an army for the defence of my people and country, that army must be paid for by his subjects. If you do not send*

*me that money speedily, then make ready a large house for me,*
*for I shall sit down and receive the revenue and custom duties,*
*as there is none to stop my passage."*

While Shivaji had been attacking Surat, he had at the same time sent a force under Moro Trimbak Pingle to Khandesh and Baglana. Here too the Mughals were prevented from resisting this invasion by Maharaja Jaswant Singh who had beseiged the Mughal governor of Khandesh in Burhanpur fort, and had demanded the payment of 5 lakh rupees in the name of Shahzada Muazzam! Another Maratha force under Pratap Rao was sent into Berar, which sacked the rich town of Karinja.

These two Maratha armies then united (25,000 strong) and besieged the fort of Salhir—on 5th January 1671 they scaled the walls with rope-ladders and slew the qiladar Fathullah Khan. By this time Mahabat Khan had reached Burhanpur, where he took away Jaswant Singh, and marched to the Chandor Range. Here a force under Daud Khan had besieged Ahivant—the Mughals captured this fort in February. Mahabat then spent several months in suspicious inactivity—Aurangzeb in anger recalled him to court and sent Bahadur Khan in his place. Dilir Khan was also sent back to the Deccan to support this new commander.

In December 1671 these two generals invaded Shivaji's kingdom—Dilir Khan captured Puna and engaged in a bloody massacre of its mostly civilian inhabitants over the age of 9. Another army under Ikhlas Khan had advanced to Salhir where Shivaji himself fought in a tough battle—it ended with the destruction of the Mughal army and the captivity of its generals. Shivaji's boyhood friend, Surya Rao Kakre, was the only chief killed on the

Maratha side. This triumph freed up the Maratha army and forced Bahadur and Dilir to withdraw from Puna.

Elevated by this succession of triumphs the Marathas continued the war even in the summer. They conquered Jawhar from its Koli Raja in June and another Koli state Ramnagar in July.

Jadun Rao, a Maratha officer in Mughal service, was defeated at Nasik that same month. But the Maratha raid into Berar and Khandesh (Oct-Dec) was defeated by the Mughals. That same year Bajaji Nayak Nimbalkar, whose son Mahadji was married to Shivaji's daughter, was won over by the Mughals and joined their service with his family.

## Path to Sovereignity (1673-74)

Ali Adil Shah II died in November 1672 and his Sultanate of Bijapur collapsed into disorder with infighting among the factions of the nobility. Shivaji sent Pratap Rao into Bijapur to loot Hubli and other towns (June 1673). In October Shivaji himself, at the command of a 25,000 strong force, entered Bijapur and sacked many towns till December. In Maharashtra he gained the forts of Panhala and Satara by bribing their Mughal commandants— however the same attempt on Shivner, his birthplace, ended in failure.

The Bijapur forces retaliated on the Maratha ruler by attacking Panhala—at the same time (Jan 1674) Dilir Khan attempted to invade the fertile Konkan belt. But Shivaji, fighting a defensive campaign, broke all the roads and hill paths and blocked every mountain pass with stones— in attempting to storm one such pass Dilir Khan was defeated with the loss of 1000 of his Pathans.

*Fig.: Panhala Fort*

By April 1674 the rising of the frontier Pathans had become so serious that Aurangzeb had to leave Delhi and take command of the operations. The best generals and men were called up for the emperor's support, including Jaswant Singh and Mahabat Khan. Dilir Khan too was called to northwest India with his force—leaving only Bahadur Khan in the Deccan. Shivaji utilized the lull in fighting to crown himself at Raigarh on 6 June 1674 with the title of *Chhatrapati,* or sovereign ruler.

## Political Geography of Peninsular India

Throughout the 17th century the central theme in the history of Peninsular India was the invasion, and rapid expansion, of the northern Mughal Empire.

Deccan Sultanates like Khandesh and Ahmadnagar had been consumed in this advance—now only the Sultanates of Bijapur and Golconda remained—both ruled by Shias.

The Mughal territory in the peninsula covered the modern Indian states of Maharashtra, parts of Karnataka, and parts of Andhra Pradesh. Golconda territory was in the eastern parts of Andhra Pradesh while Bijapur lands covered Karnataka and portions of Maharashtra—into this equation came Shivaji.

While these big powers clashed, he quietly built up his state along the western parts of Maharashtra, covering the Konkan coast, the Sahyadri range, and parts of the plateau land bordering the hills (called *Desh* in Marathi).

This early expansion had come at the expense of the Sultan of Bijapur, overlord of Shivaji's father.

Other minor powers with whom Shivaji came in conflict were the local Maratha, Koli, and Bhil states in the Sahyadri Hills, the Siddis of Janjira, and the Portuguese in Goa.

Their ambitions curbed in the north by the Mughals, Bijapur and Golconda turned their energies south. This fertile land forming the modern Indian states of Tamil Nadu and southern Karnataka, was covered by the numerous fragments of the ancient Kingdom of Vijaynagar, ruled by petty Rajas, Polygars, and Nayaks.

*Fig.: Map of The Sultanates of Deccan [Courtesy: maps of india.com]*

The Sultans themselves could not lead this war of expansion, because of their moral decay and the ever-present threat of a Mughal attack. Instead the south was invaded by officers of the two sultanates, one of these being Shahaji the father of Shivaji.

## Maratha gains (1674-76)

The lavish coronation ceremony exhausted Shivaji's treasury and he needed money to pay his troops. At the height of the monsoon season in July 1674, when the Deccan armies usually went into cantonments, a force of 2000 Maratha cavalry attacked Bahadur Khan at his base in Pedgaon. The Mughal viceroy came out with his army and chased the wily Marathas—unknown to him Shivaji with the main force of 7000 horsemen swooped down on Pedgaon from *another* direction and thoroughly looted the Mughal army's camp. On this occasion Shivaji is said to have taken away almost a crore in booty and 200 fine horses meant for the emperor.

In October 1674 Maratha bands attempted to make another attack on Surat but their passage was blocked in the jungles and hills of Ramnagar by 3000 Bhils—the latter even spurned a bribe of 1 lakh rupees for giving safe passage to the Marathas. That same month Shivaji roved through Baglana and Khandesh, defeating Qutbuddin Khan Kheshgi with the loss of 300 men. In February 1675 a Mughal force entered the Sahyadri Range and sacked the town of Kalyan, where they set fire to the houses, including those of the Ismaili Khoja traders.

Later that year Shivaji's men besieged the Portuguese fort of Ponda—to gain time for this siege to be completed Shivaji opened negotiations with Bahadur Khan. The viceroy, tired of a relentless war with no hope of reinforcements, eagerly forwarded the terms of Shivaji's "submission" to Aurangzeb far in the northwest. The latter sent back a *farman* accepting these terms—but by that time (July) Ponda had been captured and Shivaji scornfully addressed the Mughal envoys holding out the farman, *"What pressure have you succeeded in putting on me that I should seek peace with you? Go away quickly, or you will be disgraced!"*

After the rains, Bahadur Khan, pressed by the infuriated Aurangzeb, again attacked Kalyan. In January 1676 a Maratha band created a diversion into Aurangabad but Bahadur chased them down with a light force—around this time Shivaji was struck by illness for three months. In May Moro Trimbak Pingle defeated the Raja of Ramnagar and captured Pindval and Panva.

## Lure of the South (1676-78)

The eruption of a bloody faction fight at Bijapur created a new opportunity for Bahadur Khan—like all Mughal viceroys in the Deccan he relished the money that could be made in looting the settled lands of Bijapur than in trudging through the fortified hills of Shivaji's poorer realm. Knowing this Shivaji made an agreement with Bahadur Khan—his envoy Niraji Ravji paid a large bribe (in secret) to the Mughal viceroy with another sum as tribute to Aurangzeb.

Shivaji promised not to intervene in or take advantage of the projected Mughal invasion of Bijapur—on his part Shivaji asked Bahadur Khan for neutrality during his own campaign..... *in the south*! With the main Mughal forces still engaged in the northwest, Bijapur in shambles, and Bahadur Khan preparing to loot that state, Shivaji had a golden opportunity of bypassing these powers and enriching himself in the chequered lands in the south. For this purpose, and unknown to Bahadur Khan, Shivaji also formed an understanding with the Golconda Sultan.

Even more than Bijapur, it was the weaker Sultanate of Golconda that feared annexation by the Mughals. Their Brahmin minister Madanna had already formed a subsidiary alliance with Shivaji for protecting Golconda from a Mughal invasion. Now Shivaji sought their cooperation in his project, promising them a portion of the loot gained. The Sultan Abul Hassan Qutb Shah agreed to pay Shivaji 4.5 lakh rupees a month, send a 5000 strong army under his *sar-i-lashkar* Mirza Muhammad Amin, and provide Shivaji with much needed artillery and munitions.

Shivaji set out from Raigarh in January 1677 and reached Hyderabad in February at the head of a 60,000 strong army (mostly cavalry). With his Golconda allies Shivaji entered the fertile plains of Tamil Nadu and in two months captured several big and small forts, including the famous Gingee and Vellore—this Gingee later became famous as the capital of the Maratha resistance to the Mughals. Shivaji also arranged for the erection of more forts in this region.

*Fig.: Gingee Fort*

The financial results of this venture were considerable and are reported in the official exchanges of the English East India Company as follows, *"With a success as happy as Caeser's in Spain, he came, saw and overcame, and reported so vast a treasure in gold, diamonds, emeralds, rubies, and wrought coral that have strengthened his arms with very able sinews to prosecute his further designs."*

Shivaji next entered the Mysore plateau in November 1677 where he conquered Sera, Kopal, Gadag, and

Lakshmishwar. In January 1678 he had marched north into the Belgaum region....by this time the war against the frontier Pathans was over and Mughal forces were once again pouring into the Deccan.

## Changing Alliances (1676-77)

The nobility and army of Bijapur was divided into numerous factions—Afghans, Ethiopians, and Deccani Muslims at the capital—apart from the indigenous vassals like the Marathas and Berads in the countryside.

Of these the Afghans had grown to form almost half the Bijapur army—from constant migrations and desertion from Mughal service. The others naturally grouped together to fight these Afghans but were defeated in 1676—many of them took refuge with the Mughal viceroy Bahadur Khan.

Eager to win loot in the disturbed state, Bahadur crossed the River Bhima to attack the capital city in mid-1676 but did not gain much success. He was later bolstered by the forces of the Deccani Muslims—and it was at this time that he reached the understanding with Shivaji described above. With his base now secure Bahadur renewed his attack and captured Naldurg and Gulbarga by bribery.

Unfortunately the rapid approach of the main Mughal forces freed up from the campaign in northwestern India, particularly the mercurial Dilir Khan, spoiled all the viceroy's plans of enriching himself. As an Afghan himself, Dilir fraternized with Bahlol Khan, the leader of the Bijapur Afghans—these two proposed to Aurangzeb that with their united armies they would conquer Golconda and even crush Shivaji. Aurangzeb therefore recalled Bahadur

Khan Kokaltash (Sept 1677)—the ex-viceroy's only lasting achievement was the re-naming of Pedgaon as Bahadurgarh after himself!

Dilir and Bahlol first tried to threaten Golcondaâ"demanding the fantastic sum of 1 crore rupees and 10,000 horses from the Sultan as a fine for assisting Shivaji! The Afghan army entered Golconda in August 1677, fighting many inconclusive battles, and eventually being driven out from the sultanate. The severely ill Bahlol Khan died and his men broke out in mutiny for their pay. Shivaji was then in the midst of his southern campaign. He had left behind armies under Moro Trimbak (in Desh) and Annaji Datto (in Konkan)—taking advantage of Dilir's disastrous retreat from Golconda, they raided Hubli in Sept 1677 and Nasik the following January.

## Shivaji's Return (1678-80)

Sultan Abul Hassan was quite dejected by the results of the joint Maratha-Golconda enterprise in the south. All the gains had been appropriated by Shivaji and not one of the captured forts was delivered to Golconda officers—so after repelling Dilir's Afghan invasion the Golconda Sultan arranged a peace between the Bijapuri factions. The Ethiopian Siddi Masaud would be the new regent, and he would pay off Bahlol's mutinous Afghan followers who would then be disbanded.

The Mughals too agreed to this change and signed a treaty with Masaud, making him promise that he would never make an alliance with Shivaji. A Golconda army then escorted the new regent to his capital (Feb 1678)—at this time Shivaji was passing through the western portions of Bijapur.

Seeing his enemies bogged down, Shivaji prepared for one more assault on Shivneri in April 1678—here the Marathas attempted their favourite tactic of making a night attack and scaling the hill-side and the fort walls with rope ladders. But the Mughal fort commander, Abdul Aziz Khan, was vigilant and slew those soldiers who reached the top—the next morning he hunted out the remaining Marathas from the hill-sides and sent them back to Shivaji. Failure to liberate his birthplace was one of the great disappointments of Shivaji's life.

*Fig.: Shivneri Fort*

By this time the political situation at Bijapur went through another twist—Dilir Khan accused Masaud of being secretly allied to Shivaji. He recruited the disbanded Afghan soldiers of the dead Bahlol and invaded Bijapur (Oct 1678). But just then Shivaji suffered the second great disappointment of his life—from within his own family. His erratic and temperamental son Sambhaji had been confined to Panhala Fort for some offences. In Nov 1678 he escaped and joined the Mughal general Dilir Khan, who was then approaching Bijapur.

Dilir Khan was ecstatic at gaining this important ally—in the words of a contemporary historian, *"He felt as happy as if he conquered the whole Deccan! He beat his drums in joy and sent a report to the emperor."* By a royal farman Sambhaji was given the highest rank of commander of 7000, an elephant for his personal use, and the title of Raja like his father! Dilir then made peace with Bijapur and instead attacked and captured Shivaji's fort of Bhupalgarh in April 1679.

In August he again attacked Bijapur—the Ethiopian regent Masaud sent an appeal to Shivaji, *"The condition of this royalty is not hidden from you. There is no army, money, or ally for defending the capital and no provision at all. The enemy is strong and ever bent on war....we cannot defend the kingdom and its forts without your aid. Be true to your salt, turn towards us. Command what you consider proper, and it shall be done by us."*

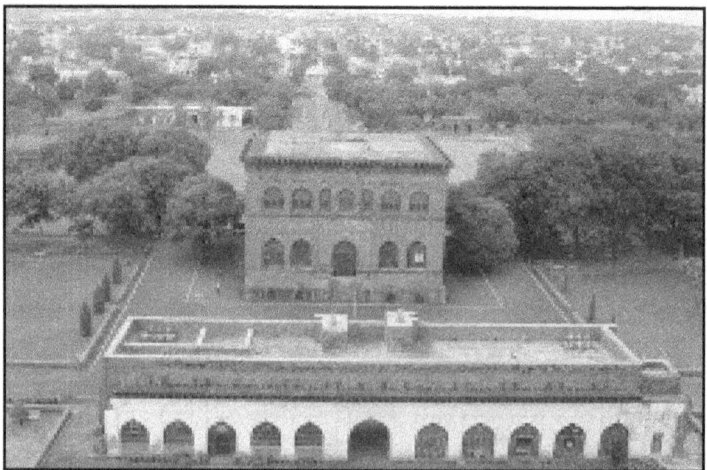

*Fig.: Modern Bijapur*

Shivaji responded to this appeal sending 10,000 Maratha cavalry (commanded by Anand Rao) and 2000 ox-loads of provisions to Bijapur—himself reaching Bijapur with another force (8,500 cavalry). These two divisions then attacked Mughal territory from diferent directions, plundering the estates of the Mughal officers, and raiding across a vast swathe of land. Dilir retaliated by an attack on Maratha lands in the Miraj-Panhala belt, where Sambhaji promised that many local officers and men would join him. But Sambhaji wasn't aware of Dilir's fondness for ill-treating civilians—the village of Tikota was sacked and its inhabitants were enslaved.

Again at Athni Dilir proposed to sell off the captured civilians into slavery—Sambhaji raised objections to this vile act but was over-ruled. Disgusted by the Mughal attitude the Maratha prince escaped to Bijapur on 21 November 1679 and was escorted by his father's men back to Panhala.

Ultimately Dilir's invasion of Bijapur failed and he took revenge on the vassal-states of Bijapur, slaying people indiscriminately, till he was defeated by the Berads of Sagar (1680). Shivaji's men too, after initial successes, suffered defeats at the hands of the Mughals and were forced to retire to their forts—but now events in North India overshadowed the affairs of the Deccan.

## Shivaji's Last Days

Aurangzeb's attempts to annex Jodhpur, the largest Hindu Kingdom in North India, and impose the *jaziya* tax on the Hindu population (April 1679), had caused the outbreak of a wider war against the Rajputs. Shivaji had been moved to send a letter to Aurangzeb protesting against the imposition of this bigoted tax. But the war did not go well for Aurangzeb and he was forced to call on all the resources of the Mughal Empire—including the generals in the Deccan to his aid in Rajputana. By early 1680 the Mughal Deccan was empty of troops.

Shivaji used this lull in fighting to reason with his wayward son. He showed Sambhaji the list of all his forts, the numerous armies, and the rich treasury, all of which were a splendid base for a new Hindu Kingdom in the south after the break-up of Vijaynagar less than a century ago. But there was also a conflict between his wives for the succession to the throne. With these domestic tensions plaguing him, Shivaji passed away on the 24th March, 1680.

## Afzal Khan (general)

Afzal Khan (died 10 November 1659) was a medieval Indian commander who served the Adil Shahi dynasty of Bijapur, and fought against the Marathas. He was killed by the Marathas at a meeting with Shivaji, and his army was defeated in the Battle of Pratapgad.

He is also referred to as "Afzul Khan" or "Afzal Khan Adilshahi" in the historical records.

### Early Life

*Fig.: Ali Adil Shah II appointed Afzal Khan the Adilshahi as the mansabdar of the elite 10,000 army of Bijapur.*

Afzal Khan was a leading court figure during the reign of Ali Adil Shah II of the Bijapur Sultanate. His steadfast skills and commanding ability led to his popularity and emergence in the ranks of hierarchy. According to legend he was awarded a famous sword known as the *Adili*, the sword was studded with diamonds. Afzal Khan was also given a popular elephant Howdah named *Dhal-Gaj*. He was also given the title *Mansabdar of 10,000*.

## War against the Marathas

When the Maratha rebels led by Shivaji challenged the Adilshahi supremacy, Afzal Khan volunteered to the task of defeating the Marathas. According to a Bijapuri legend, he sought a Sufi Pir's blessings before setting out on every military campaign. On such a visit before the campaign against Shivaji, the elderly Pir prophesied that it would be Afzal Khan's last campaign.

In 1659, Afzal Khan led an army of about 10,000 elite troops and pursued Shivaji persistently, inflicting numerous casualties, which forced Shivaji's forces to take refuge in the hill forts.

In a bid to force Shivaji to come out in open, he detoured to desecrate Hindu sacred places, including Pandharpur, the most important pilgrimage site in the Marathi-speaking region at the time. Such behaviour was unprecedented for a Bijapuri forces, and alienated the local deshmukhs (revenue collectors). He also captured Tuljapur, where his Adilshahi forces razed the statue of the Hindu Goddess Bhavani.

Afzal Khan's original plan was to invade Pune, Shivaji's original residence. Shivaji knew that he would not be able to defeat Afzal Khan in the plains, and moved to Pratapgad Fort, which was surrounded by the dense forest valley area of Jawali. Shivaji's army excelled in this type of terrain, which made the Adilshahi army's cannons, muskets, elephants, horses and camels ineffective. At the same time, Shivaji had limited stores inside the fort and Afzal Khan's raids had caused terror among his followers. Afzal Khan also attempted to garner support from local militarily independent landlords of Pratapgad, who nominally acknowledged the suzerainty of the Adil Shahi.

Afzal Khan felt that the ensuing battle would cause massive casualties to both sides and eventually lead to a deadly stalemate. He, therefore, sent out emissaries to Shivaji, to lure him down the fort and negotiate peace. Shivaji's council also urged him to make peace with Afzal Khan to avoid unnecessary losses. The two leaders, therefore, agreed to meet for negotiations.

In 1639, Afzal Khan had murdered Raja Kasturi Ranga after inviting him for a meeting where he could safely make a submission. Therefore, Shivaji was wary of Afzal Khan's real intentions. When Afzal Khan sent his envoy Krishnaji Bhaskar to Shivaji, Shivaji solemnly appealed to him as a Hindu priest to tell him if Afzal Khan was making any treacherous plans. According to the Maratha chronicles, Krishnaji hinted that Afzal Khan harbored mischief.

Shivaji then sent his own envoy Pantaji Gopinath to Afzal, agreeing to a meeting; Pantaji's real mission was to find out the strength of Afzal's forces. Pantaji bribed some officials of Afzal Khan to learn that he was planning an attack on Shivaji. Afzal Khan had originally asked Shivaji to meet him at Wai. Warned by Pantaji, Shivaji insisted that the meeting should take place closer to Pratapgad.

Afzal Khan agreed, on the condition that the meeting would be arranged with two personal bodyguards on each side. His forces marched to Par, a village lying one mile south of Pratapgad. A crest below Pratapgad was chosen as the meeting place. Shivaji set up tents with a richly-decorated canopy at the place, but also placed his soldiers in ambush at various intervals on the path leading to the meeting place. The powerful nobleman Kanhoji

Jedhe, as directed by Shivaji's father Shahaji, helped Shivaji formulate a plot to murder Afzal Khan.

*Death*

It was agreed that the leaders would be unarmed, and each man would bring an envoy and two armed bodyguards: one would be a swordsman and another an archer. Afzal Khan's companions included Sayyid Banda, who was regarded the best swordsman in the whole of Deccan at that time.

Shivaji, forewarned, wore armour under his clothes and a steel helmet under his turban. He carried a weapon called *wagh nakh* ("tiger claws"), consisting of an iron finger-grip with four razor claws, which he concealed within his clenched fist. He also carried a stiletto-like thin dagger called the *bichu* or Bichawa (scorpion). He was accompanied by his bodyguards Shambuji Kavji and Jiva Mahala.

At the start of the meeting Afzal Khan graciously embraced Shivaji as per custom. According to the Maratha chronicles, he then suddenly tightened his clasp, gripped Shivaji's neck in his left arm and struck him with a kitar. Shivaji, saved by his armor, recovered and counter-attacked Afzal Khan with *wagh nakh*, disemboweling him. He then stabbed Khan with his *bichwa*, and ran out of the tent towards his men. The Persian language chronicle by Khafi Khan attributes the treachery to Shivaji instead.

Afzal Khan cried out and Sayyid Banda rushed to the scene and attacked Shivaji with his patta, cutting his turban. Shivaji's bodyguard Jiva Mahala intervened, chopping off Sayeed Banda' s right arm in a quick combat before killing him. Meanwhile, Afzal Khan's bearers placed their wounded leader in his palki (litter vehicle), but they were attacked by Sambhaji Kavji. Sambhaji eventually killed Afzal Khan by decapitating him.

Shivaji then reached the Pratapgad Fort, and signaled his waiting forces hiding in surrounding forest, to launch a surprise attack.

Afzal Khan's army was routed in subsequent Battle of Pratapgad, though his son managed to escape. Later, severed head of Afzal Khan was sent to Rajgad as exhibit to Jijabai, Shivaji's mother. Later on, Shivaji also exhibit the fingers of the Mughal Nawab, Shaista Khan to Jijabai. The story of the encounter between Afzal Khan and Shivaji is the subject of several films, plays, school textbooks and village ballads in Maharashtra.

*Personality*

Afzal Khan was a powerful man of Afghan descent and was an experienced warrior. He was a tall of a man rumored to be about 7 feet and built proportionally to his height. He towered over everyone including the relatively short Shivaji, whose head reached only the chest of Afzal Khan.

Afzal Khan was known for his physical strength. During his campaign against Shivaji, one of his cannons fell into a narrow ditch near Wai. Eight of his soldiers could not get it out (lack of manoeuvrable space was one of the causes).

It is said that Afzal Khan got the cannon out single-handed. Another instance of Afzal Khan's strength is when he held Shivaji's head in his grip while trying to stab him. Shivaji almost lost consciousness because of the power of the grip. Later, it was discovered that the steel helmet worn by Shivaji was bent.

*Aftermath*

Shivaji had Afzal Khan buried with full military honors, as befitting his stature and reputation at the foot of the Pratapgad fort. Afzal Khan's mausoleum still exists today, where an annual *urs* is held.

Afzal Khan was succeeded by the inexperienced Rustam Zaman and Siddi Masud. The Bijapuri forces had been completely weakened, and eventually sought the assistance of the Mughal Emperor Aurangzeb. The Adilshahi dynasty of Bijapur did not last long after the killing of Afzal Khan and was eventually annexed during the Siege of Bijapur in 1686. His servicemen included: Fazal Khan (his son), Musa Khan, Manoji Jagdale, Sardar Pandhare, Ambar Khan, the Abyssinian Rustam-i-Zaman II and even Bari Sahiba the wife of the ruler of Bijapur.

❑❑❑

# Chapter 8

# Battle of Pratapgarh

The Battle of Pratapgad was a land battle fought on November 10, 1659 at the fort of Pratapgad near the town of Satara, Maharashtra, India between the forces of the Maratha king Shivaji and the Adilshahi general Afzal Khan. The Marathas defeated the Adilshahi forces despite being outnumbered. It was their first significant military victory against a major regional power, and led to the eventual establishment of the Maratha Empire.

Shivaji held a commendable position in parts of Maval. The Adilshahi court wanted to curb his activities. Afzal Khan, a renowned general of Bijapur who had previously killed Shivaji's brother in a battle treacherously, was selected to lead an assault against Shivaji. He started from Bijapur in June 1659.

> [Maval or (Mawal) is a tehsil in Maval subdivision of Pune district in the Indian state of Maharashtra. The word Maval is derived from a Marathi word *Mavalati*, meaning the direction in which the sun sets. This region is towards the west of Pune area. It is hilly terrain and part of the Sahyadri range/ western ghats. The Sahyadri range goes from north

to south. On the western part of the range lies the Konkan area and on the eastern side 'Maval'. Many rivers originate from this region and travel from west to east.

Broadly speaking maval is subdivided into 12 subregions. Each subregion is mostly identified by the name of a river. The names of the subregions are Nane maval, Andar maval, Pawan maval, Gunjan maval, Karyat maval, Kanand maval, Hirdus maval, Mose Maval, Velkhand Maval etc. The highest point of this region is the Mahabaleshwar area, which is approximately 4500 feet above sea level. Maval is one of the world's highly biodiversified regions. It was the first abode of Shivaji, who formed an army of the local peasants called 'Mavale'. Chhatrapati Shivaji united, motivated, empowered and trained the 'mavale'. Maval region is a home to numerous forts of significant historical military importance. The whole of this region proudly carries the historical footprints of the Great Shivaji and his loyal 'Mavale'.]

## Battle

After starting from Bijapur, Afzal Khan began by destroying the temple of Bhavani at Tuljapur. He moved on to the Vittal temple at Pandharpur. He was trying to entice Shivaji out of the mountainous areas he occupied and onto the plains, where Khan's larger army trained and equipped for warfare on plain grounds would have an absolute advantage. Shivaji had encamped at Pratapgad, which, being located in a hilly area, was strategically advantageous for mountainous guerrilla warfare.

Unable to incite him to attack first, Afzal Khan moved his army to Pratapgad. As he had once been the subedar of Wai, he had experience with the geography of the region. He tried to bolster his position by obtaining the support of the militarily independent landlords of the region. Although they nominally acknowledged the sovereignty of the Adilshah, the powerful baron Kanhoji Jedhe, as directed by Shahaji, helped Shivaji to counter these moves and garner their support.

## Composition of Adilshahi Forces

Afzal Khan was assisted by the chieftains Sayyad Banda, Fazal Khan, Ambarkhan, Yakutkhan, Siddi Hilal, Musekhan, Pilaji Mohite, Prataprao More and many more commanders of note. His forces consisted of 12,000 select Adilshahi cavalry, 10,000 infantry and 1,500 musketeers. He was accompanied by 85 elephants and 1,200 camels. His artillery consisted of 80-90 cannons. Siddi of Janjira was approaching from the Konkan coast.

## Composition of Maratha Forces

Shivaji was assisted by Kanhoji Jedhe along with other Deshmukhs of Maval region namely Maral, Ramoji Dhamale, Silimkar and Bandal. His cavalry was commanded by Netaji Palkar, and were placed in a forward position near the fort. Moropant Pingle was in command of 3,000 chosen infantry men, who were positioned in a densely forested area. Sambhaji Kavaji Kondhalkar, Yesaji Kank, Jiva Mahala and many other skilled military leaders were in charge of them. Kanhoji Jedhe assisted Shivaji directly along with other commanders. In the meantime, Shahaji was ready in Bangalore with his army of 17,000 for a final Battle in case Shivaji and his forces were routed by Khan. He had warned Badi Begum of Adilshah that, if Afzal Khan and his Adilshahi forces killed Shivaji by deceit, then there wouldn't remain even a brick of the Adilshahi kingdom. These forces were being carefully watched by the Adilshah.

[Kanhoji Jedhe was a 17th-century Marathi warrior, and a trusted follower of Shahaji, and of Shahaji's son Shivaji who founded the Maratha Empire in 1674. Kanhoji came from a village named Kari, in present day Bhor taluka, near Pune. He was respected among the Deshmukhs, noblemen in the area. Kanhoji was some 20 years older than Shivaji. Shahaji sent Kanhoji along with the young Shivaji to Pune. Because of his high personal standing among the Jamindars, he helped Shivaji Maharaj in organising most of them under his banner.

His actual testing time came when Afzal Khan, a Sardar sent by Bijapur court, came to attack Shivaji. Adilshah had threatened all the Deshmukhs of the Maval region to support Afzal or else perish. Kanhoji not only stood by Shivaji, but managed to keep nearly all the Deshmukhs on Shivaji Maharaj's side. After Afzal was defeated soundly at the Battle of Pratapgad, Shivaji Maharaj honored the loyalty and bravery of Kanhoji by awarding him *talwarichya pahilya panache maankari* (Sword of Honour).

Kanhoji demonstrated his own magnanimity after the Battle of Pavan Khind. Immediately after Afzul Khan's death during the encounter with Shivaji Maharaj, Siddi Jauhar, a great warrior, was sent to defeat Shivaji. To protect the citizens of the

Maratha Empire, Shivaji decided to stay at Panhala Fort (near Kolhapur) which was at the boundary so that Siddi Jauhar's attack would not take him into the territory. Jauhar then surrounded Panhala with an army of forty thousand. When all other attempts to break Jauhar's siege failed, Shivaji decided to escape secretly. In the monsoon season, Shivaji and a small escort of soldiers crossed the siege line one night during heavy rain. However, Jauhar's army soon realized that he had escaped, and Jauhar sent soldiers under Siddi Masoud to catch Shivaji.

After more than half a day's pursuit Siddi Masoud came very close to Shivaji and his escort. Then Baji Prabhu Deshpande, a senior warrior with Shivaji, convinced Shivaji to continue his travel towards Vishalgad while Baji Prabhu along with few warriors of Bandal clan held the narrow passage called Ghod-khind (Horse Pass). Baji Prabhu and his men fought with Jauhar's army and prevented them from crossing the pass. When Shivaji reached fort Vishalgad, defeating Surve Sawant's siege, he notified Baji Prabhu by firing three cannon shots.

By now Baji Prabhu and his army were tired as they had been fighting for more than six hours, and Baji Prabhu had suffered many wounds. He died shortly after hearing the three cannon shots, realizing that Shivaji Maharaj had reached safety at Vishalgad. Shivaji was very sad to lose such a brave and loyal warrior. To honor Baji Prabhu, he wished to give the honor of *talwarichya pahilya panache maankari* – which had been held by Kanhoji after Afzal's defeat – to Baji Prabhu's Bandal clan.

When Shivaji expressed this desire to Kanhoji, he agreed to it without hesitation. This was a great deed by Kanhoji, considering the fact that Kanhoji Jedhe and the Bandal clan had been great enemies until a few years before this incident.

Kanhoji Jedhe also played a pivotal part in bringing Shivaji back from Agra where he was under house arrest. In the 20th century, the descendants of Kanhoji Jedhe also played a leading role in the establishment of the State of Maharashtra; Samyukta Maharashtra Samiti, founded by Keshavrao Jedhe, led the demand for a the Marathi-speaking state. Maharashtra was formed as a direct result of this Samiti; the Hutatma Chowk and Maharashtra Day commemorate the relentless efforts of the Jedhes.]

## Combat of Shivaji and Afzal Khan

Shivaji sent an emissary to Afzal Khan, stating that he did not want to fight and was ready for peace. A meeting was arranged between Shivaji and Afzal Khan at a shamiyana (highly decorated tent) at the foothills of Pratapgad. It was agreed that the two would meet unarmed, but would bring ten personal bodyguards each. Nine of these guards would remain 'one arrow-shot' away from the pair, while a single bodyguard would wait outside the tent. Shivaji Maharaj chose Sambhaji Kondhalkar, Jiva Mahala, Siddi Ibrahim, Kataji Ingle, Kondaji Kank, Yesaji Kank, Krishnaji Gayakwad, Surji Katake, Visaji Murambak & Sambhaji Karvar for the meet. Nevertheless, both were prepared for treachery: Afzal Khan hid a katyar (a small dagger) in his coat, and Shivaji wore armour underneath his clothes and carried a concealed *wagh nakhi* in one hand.

As the two men entered the tent, the 7' tall Khan embraced Shivaji. Then treacherous Khan swiftly drew his hidden dagger and stabbed Shivaji in the back. The dagger was deflected by Shivaji's armour. Brave Shivaji responded by disemboweling the Khan with a single stroke of his *wagh nakhi*. Khan rushed outside shouting for help, and was defended by Krishanaji Bhaskar Kulkarni, his emissary, who was himself then killed by Shivaji.

Kulkarni managed to injure Shivaji. Thereupon Afzal Khan's bodyguard Sayyed Banda attacked Shivaji with swords but Jiva Mahala, Shivaji's personal bodyguard fatally struck him down, cutting off one of Sayyed Banda's hands with a Dandpatta (Pata- a medieval weapon). (This event is remembered in a Marathi idiom: *Hota Jiva Mhanun Vachala Shiva* - 'Because there was Jiva, Shiva lived').

Afzal Khan managed to hold his gushing entrails and hurtled, faint and bleeding, outside the tent and threw himself into his palanquin. The bearers hastily lifted their charge and began moving rapidly away down the slope. Sambhaji Kavji Kondhalkar, Shivaji's lieutenant and one of the accompanying guards, gave chase and beheaded Afzal Khan.

The severed head was later sent to Rajgad to be shown to Shivaji's mother, Jijabai. She had long wanted vengeance for the deliberate maltreatment of Shahaji (Shivaji's father) while a captive of Afzal Khan, and for his role in the death of her elder son, Sambhaji. Shivaji sped up the slope towards the fortress and his lieutenants ordered cannons to be fired. It was a signal to his infantry, hidden in the densely forested valley, to raid the Adilshahi forces.

## Hand to Hand Combat of the Forces

Maratha troops commanded by Shivaji's captain Kanhoji Jedhe, swept down on Afzal Khan's 1,500 musketeers; resulting in a complete rout of the musketeers at the foothills of the fort. Then in a rapid march, a section of Adilshahi forces commanded by Musekhan was attacked. Musekhan, Afzal Khan's lieutenant, was wounded and subsequently fled the field.

Meanwhile, Moropant led the Maratha infantry toward the left flank of Adilshahi troops. The suddenness of this attack on Afzal Khan's artillery at close quarters made them ineffective in providing artillery cover for the main portion of their troops. And as a result of this the rest of their troops rapidly succumbed to an all out Maratha attack. Simultaneously Shivaji's Sardar (captain), Ragho Atre's cavalry units swooped down and attacked the large but unprepared Adilshahi cavalry before they were able to be fully geared up for battle and succeeded in completely routing them in short order.

The Maratha cavalry under Netaji Palkar pursued the retreating Adilshahi forces, who were attempting to join up with the part of their reserve forces stationed in the nearby village of Wai. They were engaged in battle before they could regroup and were defeated prior to reaching Wai. The Adilshahi forces not withstanding the onslaught of the Marathas started retreating towards Bijapur. The Maratha army chased the retreating army and on their way captured 23 Adilshahi forts. In fact, the Adilshahi *Killedar* of the Kolhapur fort himself handed over the keys to the Marathas.

[Netaji Palkar was the second *Sardar Senapati* or *Sarnaubat* (Commander-in-Chief, Duke) of the Maratha Empire under Chatrapati Shivaji, the founder of the Maratha empire. Netaji's father was in the services of Shivaji's father Shahaji. Shivaji's 3rd queen Putalabai was also from Palkar's family. Netaji Palkar's birth place was a small village in Khalapur, Maharashtra, India.

During the period of the rise of Shivaji from 1645 to 1665, Netaji was given charge of many expeditions which he successfully completed. His greatest success was the campaign against the Adilshah of Bijapur that followed the killing of Afzal Khan. His standing among the local population was such that he was known as *Prati Shivaji* (Image of Shivaji). After an agreement of Mirza Raja Jai Singh and Shivaji, Shivaji was made to give 23 forts to the Mughals and also fight against the Adilshah of Bijapur. During this period, Netaji Palkar, as a tactic joined the Bijapur forces and weakened the Mughals by counter-attacking them using Adilshah's army. In turn, Shivaji used Mirzaraja Jai Singh's army to weaken the Adilshahi.

After Shivaji's meeting with Aurangzeb at Agra, Netaji Palkar joined the service of Mirza Raja Jaisingh. When Shivaji escaped from Agra, Mirza Raje fell out of favour of Aurangzeb.

After Shivaji's escape from Agra, Aurangzeb, as a revenge, ordered Mirza Raja Jai Singh I to arrest Netaji Palkar. He was then converted to Islam. His wives were thereafter brought to Delhi and also converted for him to remarry them in the Islamic way. Taking up the name of Muhammed Kuli Khan, Netaji Palkar was appointed as Garrison commander of the Kandahar fort. He tried to escape but was traced and trapped at Lahore. Thereafter on the battlefields of Kandhar and Kabul, he fought for the Mughals against rebel Pathans. Thus he gained the good faith of Aurangzeb and was sent to the Deccan along with Commander Diler Khan to conquer Shivaji's territory.

However, after entering Maharashtra, Netaji joined Shivaji's troops and went to Raigad. Thus, after a decade in Mughal captivity, Netaji turned up at the court of Shivaji, asking to be taken back into the Hindu fold.

Shivaji arranged for the reconversion of Netaji at Raigad, even though it was opposed by some of the orthodox Brahmins. However, with the acceptance and counsel of judges and senior members in Shivaji's court, he became a Hindu once more. Netaji led battles against the Adilshah at Panhala, Shahapur, Tikota and Vijapur in 1660 and at Khatav, Mangalvedha, Phaltan, Taathvada and Vijapur in 1665.]

*Aftermath*

Adilshahi forces lost their artillery, 65 elephants, 4000 horses, 1200 camels, jewels worth 300,000 Rupees, 1,000,000 Rupees, heaps of precious cloths, tents to the Marathas. They also lost their money and grain stored at Wai.

5,000 Adilshahi soldiers were killed and almost as many were wounded. 3,000 soldiers were imprisoned, and the remainder were allowed to go home in defeat. The Marathas lost 1,734 soldiers, while 420 soldiers were wounded.

As it was policy of Shivaji to humanely treat the defeated army, neither the men nor women were sold as slaves or molested. Wounded commanders were offered treatment deserving of their rank and either imprisoned or sent back to Bijapur. Some of the defeated Adilshahi generals like Siddi Hilal changed their loyalties and joined the Marathas to serve under Shivaji Maharaj. Two of Afzal khan's sons were captured by the Marathas but were let off by the Shivaji Maharaj. Fazal khan (son of Afzal khan) and the Adilshahi soldiers with him who were badly injured were shown a safe passage out of the forest of Jawli by Prataprao More.

The sword of honour was presented to Kanhoji Jedhe for his invaluable and outstanding performance of service to Shivaji. The relatives of the killed soldiers were offered service in the Maratha army. Families without any male left alive to support the family were awarded pensions. Heroes of the war were rewarded with medals, kada (bracelets) and horses.

Khan's death dealt the Adilshah's rule a severe blow. A quarter of his territory, forts and a fifth of his army were captured or destroyed, while Shivaji doubled his territory, losing a tenth of his army, within fifteen days of the Battle of Pratapgadh.Shivaji maintained his momentum, sending cavalry towards Kolhapur, which succeeded in capturing seventeen forts, including the prestigious fort of Panhala. Cavalry was also sent towards Dabhol and Rajapur under the command of Doroji Patil, which was also successful in capturing forts in the southern Konkan. This remarkable victory made Shivaji a hero of Maratha folklore and a legendary figure among his people.

Having established military dominance and successfully beaten back a major attack by a powerful empire, Shivaji had founded the nucleus of what would become the Maratha Empire.

□□□

# Chapter 9

# Battle of Kolhapur

Battle of Kolhapur was a land battle that took place on December 28, 1659 near the city of Kolhapur, Maharashtra, India between the Maratha *Chhatrapati* Shivaji and the Rustam Zaman of Adilshah. The Marathas defeated the Adilshahi forces. Adilshahi forces were 10000 strong against 5000 light Maratha cavalry.

> [Rustam Zaman was a Bijapuri general who commanded Adil Shah's 10,000 strong army, in the Battle of Kolhapur against Shivaji's forces.]

The battle is known for brilliant movement of flanks by Shivaji similar to Uzbek tactics of Babur against Rana Sangha.

Shivaji had killed Afzal Khan and routed his army in the battle of Pratapgarh (10 November 1659). He took advantage of this victory and in a great offensive took a large hilly tract running about 200 km under his command. A number of forts like Vasota fell to Marathas. By December, 1659 Shivaji appeared near Panhala fort. Rustam Zaman was directed from Bijapur. He arrived near Miraj in the vicinity of Kolhapur on 27 December 1659.

## Battle

*Composition of Adilshahi Forces*

Rustam Zaman was assisted by other chieftains Fazal Khan, Malik Itbar, Sadat Khan, Yakub Khan, Aankush Khan, Hasan Khan, Mulla Yahya, Santaji Ghatage. It consists of selected cavalry of Adilshahi which was well known.

In addition elephants were deployed as first line of defense. The centre was commanded by Rustam Zaman himself, left flank by Fazal Khan, right flank by Malik Itbar. Fateh Khan and Mullah Yahya were on the rear guard.

*Composition of Maratha Forces*

Shivaji was assisted by Maratha Cavalry leader Netaji Palkar, SARDAR GODAJIRAJE JAGTAP, Hiroji Ingale, Bhimaji Wagh, Sidhoji Pawar Jadhavrao, Hanmantrao Kharate, Pandhare, Siddi Hllal, and Mahadik.

Center was commanded by Shivaji Maharaj himself. Siddi Hilal and Jadhavrao were on left flank. Ingale and Sidhoji Pawar on right flank. Mahadik and Wagh on the rear guard. Netaji Palkar was off the centre.

*Movement and Clash of Forces*

Rustam Zaman was planning to move towards Panhala fort. Shivaji anticipated this movement and in a quick dash appeared before Adilshahi forces in the early morning of 28 December 1659. And attacked the enemy. Shivaji charged the center.

Other Maratha commanders attacked respective flanks. In a hard battle, Adilshahi forces were scuttled. By afternoon Rustam Zaman had fled the field.

## Outcome

Shivaji gained a large territory and secured front of his emerging empire. Adilshahi forces lost about 2000 horses and 12 elephants to the Marathas. The Marathas under Shivaji Maharaj continued to harass and conquer more Adilshahi territory. In one of the incidences, Shivaji tried to conquer an Adilshahi fort named *Khelna* but the terrain of the fort was difficult; conquering the fort was easier said than done. The Adilshahi garrison at the fort was also defending the fort valiantly. Then, Shivaji came up with a plan.

Accordingly, a group of Marathas went up to the fort and convinced the Adilshahi chief (*killedar*) at the fort that they were not content with the rule of Shivaji and thus, had come to serve the Adilshah. The Marathas were successful and the next day, they revolted and caused total chaos inside the fort. Simultaneously, Shivaji attacked the fort from outside and in no time captured the fort. Shivaji renamed the fort as Vishalgad.

## Casualties

The total casualties of this battle and also battle of Pratapgarh was 7000 on Adilshahi side and 2000 on Maratha side.

□□□

# Chapter 10

# Battle of Pavan Khind

Battle of Pävankhind was a rear guard battle and a Last Stand that took place on July 13, 1660 at a mountain pass in the vicinity of fort Vishalgad, near the city of Kolhapur, Maharashtra, India between the Maratha sardar Baji Prabhu Deshpande and Siddi Masud of Adilshah. The Marathas held the Adilshahi forces till Shivaji Maharaj reached the fort Vishalgad. The Adilshahi forces were 15,000 strong against 300 Maratha light infantry.

[Vishalgad (also called Khelna or Khilna) was one of the important forts of Shivaji and Maratha Empire. The name 'Vishalgad' meaning *grand fort* in Marathi, was given by Shivaji after annexing it for the Maratha Empire in 1659.The fort is about 1130 meters that is 3630 feet.

Khelna was in the control of Adilshah of Bijapur. Shivaji wanted to conquer the fort but the terrain of the fort was difficult; conquering the fort was easier said than done. Shivaji attacked the fort but the Adilshahi garrison at the fort was defending the fort valiantly. Then, Shivaji came up with a plan. Accordingly, a group of Marathas went up to the fort and convinced the Adilshahi commander (killedar) of the fort that they were not content with the rule of Shivaji and thus, had come to serve the Adilshah. The Marathas were successful and the next day, they revolted and caused total chaos inside the fort. Simultaneously, Shivaji attacked the fort from outside and in no time captured the fort. Shivaji renamed the fort as Vishalgad.

The fort is situated in Maharashtra, India. It is 76 kilometers North-West of Kolhapur, 60 kilometers north-west of Panhala fort and 18 kilometers south of Kolhapur Ratnagiri road. It is situated on the hills that divide the region into two parts viz *Amba* ghat and *Anaskura* ghat. Since it is placed on the border of the hilly portion of Sahyadri ranges and the konkan region, it got great political significance in the historical times. It was regarded as a 'Watch tower' for both the regions.

The fort has following sites nearly in ruins today except the *Dargah*.

- Amruteshwar Temple
- Shri Nrusinha Temple
- Takmak Tok
- Sati's Vrindavan
- The *Dargah* or tomb of Hazrat Malik Raihan. Thousands of Devotees visit the *Dargah* every year.
- Samadhis built in the memory of Baji Prabhu Deshpande and Phulaji Prabhu Deshpande,

who laid down their lives to protect Chhatrapati Shivaji from the clutches of Siddhi Johar while escaping from fort Panhala to Vishalgad.

History:

- The fort was constructed by the Shilahara king 'Marsinh' in 1058 A.C. Initially, he named it as 'Khilgil'
- In 1209, the then king of Seuna Yadavas of Devagiri defeated Shilaharas and captured the fort
- In 1309, Allauddin Khilji defeated King Ramchandra of the Seuna Yadavas of Devagiri and soon the fort was attached to the Khilji Dynasty
- In August 1347, the Mughal chief of the western India Hasan Gangu Bahamani became independent as a result of which the fort became a part of Bahamani Sultanat
- During 1354 to 1433, the fort was under the rule of Vijayanagar Empire
- After the fall of the Vijayanagar Empire, it was captured by a local Maratha king Shankarrao More. Therefore, the Bahamani Sultan sent troops from Bidar under the Generalship of Mahmood Gawan, his then prime Minister, to re-capture it. Gawan's officers Karnasinh Bhonsale and his son Bhimsinha captured the fort with the help of *Ghorpad* i.e. Giant monitor lizard. Thenceforth, Bhimsinha was conferred with the title *Ghorpade*.

- In 1489, Yusuf Adil Shah separated himself from the Bahamani kingdom along with the area under his command and founded his independent sultanat at Bijapur. Hence, the fort was attached to Adil Shahi sultanate.

- In 1659, Shivaji captured the fort with the help of the officers on the fort.

- In July 1660, the fort witnessed Shivaji's escape from the Adilshahi blockade around fort Panhala and the Battle of Pavan Khind. Baji Prabhu Deshpande, Shivaji's experienced General and Rango Narayan Orpe, Shivaji's young officer on the fort, defeated Adilshahi troops at Pavan Khind and Gonimooth respectively.

- After Shivaji's death, Chhatrapati Sambhaji would spend most of his times on the fort. He took initiative in renovation and reconstruction of some parts of the fortresses and gates of the fort.

- In 1689, Rajaram Chhatrapati fled to Fort Gingee in Karnataka (now Tamilnadu) from fort Panhala and thus 'Vishalgad' became an un-official capital of the Maratha empire. Ramchandra Pant Amatya from Vishalgad and Rajaram Chhatrapati from Gingee made several moves and defeated Aurangzeb with the help of Santaji, Dhanaji, Parshurampant Pratinidhi and Shankaraji Narayan Sacheev.

- During the times of Maratha Empire, Vishalgad was made capital of a large region consisting of ninety towns and villages in Kolhapur and

Ratnagiri districts. Sardesai and Sarpotdar were officers on the fort since Adilshahi times. Some of the Havaldars (Military In Charge) on the fort during Rajaram Chhatrapati to Chhatrapati Shahu's times were :

1. Trimbakji Ingawale - 3 years

2. Santaji Kathe - 9 years

3. Khandoji Karanjkar - 3 months

4. Umaji Gaikwad - 6 months

5. Shamji Rangnath Orpe Sarpotdar - 6 years

6. Vithoji Nimbalkar - 6 months

7. Malji Dalvi - 2 months

• In 1844, as a result of mutiny by the *Killedars*, British army demolished the entire fort and dismissed the officers there]

Shivaji Maharaj defeated Adilshahi generals of distinction one after the other. Hence Adilshah as last measure pulled all his resources and sent Siddi Jauhar on the expedition against Marathas.

At the same time he made correspondence with Mughals to attack Shivaji Maharaj. Accordingly, Shaista Khan attacked from Northern side towards Pune.

Siddi Jauhar laid the siege to Panhala fort. All attempts to raise the siege were failed.

Shivaji Maharaj's senapati (Commander) Netaji Palkar could not break through the siege from outside. Hence Shivaji decided to give a final battle.

But instead of suicidal attack, he followed a different strategy. A grand escape was planned to give a battle from the fort Vishalgad.

## Battle

*Composition of Adilshahi Forces*

It consisted of selected cavalry of Adilshahi which was well known under the command of Siddi Jauhar assisted by Siddi Masud and Fazal Khan. Jasvantrao Dalvi of Palavani and Surve of Sringarpur had laid siege to Vishalgarh.

*Composition of Maratha Forces*

Shivaji was assisted by his Sardar Bajiprabhu, Jadhavrao, Bandal and many more. However, the light infantry forces were limited around 600. They consisted of hardened mountaineers of maval region who had remained historically unconquered till that time.

[Baji Prabhu Deshpande was a Minister/Count (also known as *Sardar*) of Chattrapati Shivaji, founder of the Maratha empire. The well celebrated legend of Baji Prabhu is intricately linked with an important rear guard battle enabling Shivaji's escape from Panhala fort; he was the hero who sacrificed his life for his king and country.

Baji Prabhu was 15 years elder to Shivaji Maharaj, this means he was born around 1615. He belonged to Kayasta (CKP). Baji Prabhu Deshpande was born into the CKP, a caste that follows the thread ceremony (upanayana) like the Brahmins and hence called Vedadhikaris. His Original Surname was Pradhan. He was honoured by Kulkarni Hakka as per available information from modi Scripts. He was born in Shind Village Near Bhor.

Baji Prabhu Deshpande (died 1660) was one of the lieutenants (also known as sardar) of Chhatrapati

Shivaji Maharaj, founder of the Maratha empire. The legend of Baji Prabhu is intricately linked with the final battle during Shivaji's escape from Panhala fort, where he played a key role in the final battle.]

## Movement and Clash of Forces

Siddi Jauhar had laid the siege around Panhala very well, with utmost care. Firstly, Shivaji sent his *vakil* to Siddi Jauhar saying that he was ready to sign a treaty with him.

Siddi Jauhar and his army thus relaxed a bit, foreseeing that their siege going on for months together was going to end. Still, getting through the siege of about 10000 Adilshahi soldiers seemed impossible. According to the plan, on the dead of the full moon night, Shivaji passed through the siege along with some 600 men, led by Bajiprabhu Deshpande.

They were surprisingly successful and were speeding towards Vishalgad. When the enemy came to know about Shivaji's escape from Panhala, they chased and caught some portion of his troops. The caught king turned out to be an impostor of Shivaji. He was a barber, named Shiva Kashid. This heroic sacrifice gave the fleeing Maratha force some breathing space.

The enemy started the chase once again, led by Siddi Masood, son-in-law of Siddi Johar. By that time, Shivaji had reached a strategic location, Ghod Khind (Horse Pass), a gorge.

It was very narrow so as to pass only a few soldiers at a time. Bajiprabhu Deshpande, a gallant general along with 300 of his Bandal sena, took the position to defend the pass till Shivaji reached another fort, Vishalgad.

Shivaji Maharaj attacked another siege at the base of fort Vishalgad with such vigour that it was broken. Meanwhile, Baji Prabhu, his brother Fulaji and Sambhaji Jadhav successfully defended the pass with 300 soldiers.

They were fatally wounded, soldiers of Siddi Masood were taken-aback by the sight of those 300 soldiers bleeding heavily but fighting brutally with swords in both hands they kept fighting and gave up only when they heard the sound of cannons blasted by Shivaji from the fort, indicating that he had reached safely.

The pass is now known as *Pāvan Khind* - The Sacred Pass. After crossing the pass, the enemy attacked Shivaji at Fort Vishalgad. But again they were fiercely beaten by Rango Narayan Sarpotdar, Shivaji's young officer on the Fort, and repulsed with heavy losses.

## Honour

The sword of honour was given to Bandal. Shivaji personally visited the house of slain Baji Prabhu, situated in the village of Kasabe Sindh near Bhor in the Pune district.

His elder son was offered job as chief of a section. Other 7 sons were given honour of the Palkhi. Son of Slain Sambhaji Jadhav, Dhanaji Jadhav was inducted in the forces.

### Outcome

This was the last major battle between Adilshahi forces and Marathas. Hereafter Marathas were recognised as an independent power. The sacrifice of Bajiprabhu

Deshpande and Shiva Kashid is a legend in itself. Even today youths trek on the route taken by Shivaji between the forts of Panhala and Vishal Gadh.

The distance is around 70 km.

## Casualties

The total casualties of this battle were 3,000 on Adilshahi side and 300 on Maratha side.

❑❑❑

# Chapter 11

## Battle of Umberkhind

Battle of Umberkhind took place on 3 February 1661 in the mountain range of Sahyadri near the city of Pen, Maharashtra, India. The battle was fought between the Maratha under *Chhatrapati* Shivaji and the Kartalab Khan of Mughals. The Marathas defeated the Mughal forces. Mughal forces consisted of 20,000 men, while there was just 3,000 light Maratha cavalry. The battle is known for the strategic manner in which Shivaji deployed his forces and rapid movement that his cavalry was able to achieve.

On 10 November 1659, Shivaji killed Afzal Khan and routed his army in the Battle of Pratapgarh. A month later, Shivaji appeared near the Panhala fort and defeated Rustam Zaman, who was directed from Bijapur. His senapati Netaji Palkar caused havoc in the vicinity of Bijapur. Alarmed at this, Adilshah requested mughals to send forces against Shivaji.

The Mughals sent Shaista Khan with a large force against Shivaji who camped at Pune. Meanwhile, Shivaji was trapped in the siege of Panhala by Bijapuri forces under Siddi Jauhar, although he subsequently managed to escape. Shaista Khan planned to reduce Shivaji's

possessions in Konkan and deputed Kartlab khan, an
Uzbek general with a considerable force. Kartalab decided
to surprise Shivaji and chose Khanadala Ghat to move
towards Panvel.

On receiving this news, Shivaji announced that he
was moving his force towards Panvel. Learning this
through spies, Kartalab Khan decided to move by another
route and selected a less traveled path through
Tungaranya, which went to Konkan through a mountain
pass known locally as Umberkhind.

## Battle

To reach Umberkhind from Pune, Kartalab traveled
via Chinchvad, Talegaon, Vadagaon and Malavali
(roughly parallel to the present railway line). At that
point, he turned left towards Lohagad, which was a fort
on the border of the Deccan plateau and Kokan. There,
his army began the descent into the Kokan area through
the narrow pass that separates Lohagad from Visagad.
Planning to descend into Tungaranya—a dense forest
with hills on both sides—and then move through the
Umberkhind pass, before descending into Kokan proper.

It is worth noting that when the British built the
railroad between Mumbai and Pune, they chose go
through Khandala Ghat and not via Umbar Khind. The
reason for this is because Khandala Ghat, also known as
Bor Ghat, is much more open and broad than Umberkhind
and as such the ground is not as suitable for surprise
attacks. Khan had initialled planned to descend through
Bor Ghat and if he had done so, Shivaji would have a
much harder battle on his hands.

Nevertheless, Khan went through Umberkhind. He
had been forced into this course of action by Shivaji who

had ensured that Kartalab knew that he was at the base of the khind. This was the cornerstone of Shivaji's strategy. Khan was planning a secret campaign but Shivaji's spies were far more skillful. Khan had heard that Shivaji and his army would be at Kurawanda, roughly 3 miles (4.8 km) from Lonavala. But when Khan reached Kurawanda, there was no sign of Shivaji or his army. His spies brought the news that Shivaji was at Pen, at the base of the Ghat.

Naturally, Khan chose to quickly descend this mountain pass and launch a surprise attack on Shivaji. Khan was further disadvantaged by the fact that he was traveling in February when most rivers in Konkan area were dry and drinking water was scarce. Unknown to Kartalab Khan, Shivaji and his army were already in the hills that surrounded the Umberkhind where they were ready and waiting for Khan and his army to descend to the base of the pass. They were equipped with rocks and boulders in addition to the usual rifles, sabers and bows and arrows.

Although the army consisted of about 1,000 men, the entire pass was covered with dense forest and so Shivaji's army was not visible to Khan and his army. The trap was then set for Khan. Khan and his army climbed down to the base in about 4 hours and met no resistance whatsoever. As his army moved down, Shivaji and some of his men reached the top of the pass, thus effecting the envelopment of Khan's forces.

As soon as Khan reached the base of the pass, Shivaji's army began the battle, rolling boulders down on Khan's men. Since Shivaji's army was on top of the hills, Khan and his army were in effect fighting an invisible army. Not only could they not see their enemy, but they were unable to retreat from it as a portion of Shivaji's army and Shivaji himself were waiting at the top of the mountain pass to cut them off. In the end, the battle was over in roughly two to three hours.

Khan had no choice but to surrender and beg for a safe passage. Shivaji's small army of 1,000 had trapped and defeated a well-equipped army of 20,000. Shivaji agreed to let Khan and his army leave Umberkhind and return to Khan's home base in Pune provided that Khan and his army left behind their equipment including their weapons, horses and food, and allowed anyone who wished to do so to join Shivaji's army.

Shivaji and his assistants inspected each person to ensure that they had followed the terms of the truce. Once Khan's army had left the battle area, Shivaji's army spent the rest of that day collecting, classifying and packing all items. Then they moved back towards Raj Gad.

### Aftermath

The battle boosted the morale of the Marathas, providing them with a psychological boost. Conversely, as a result of the defeat, the Mughals gave up their plan to conquer Konkan and changed their strategy. Encouraged by this, Shivaji attacked Shaista khan in a night assault. The Maratha casualties amounted to about 50 men killed or wounded, while the Mughals lost about 400.

❑❑❑

# Chapter 12

## Battle of Chakan

The Battle of Chakan was fought between the Maratha Empire and the Mughal Empire in the year 1660. Shaista Khan was ordered by Aurangzeb to attack Shivaji per the Mughal-Adilshahi accord. Shaista Khan, with his better equipped and provisioned army of 150,000 that was many times the size of the Maratha forces, seized Pune and the nearby fort of Chakan.

[Mirza Abu Talib, better known by his title Shaista Khan, was a *Subahdar* and general in the army of the Mughal Empire. A maternal uncle to Emperor Aurangzeb, he served as the Mughal governor of Bengal from 1664 to 1688, and was a key figure during the rule of his nephew, the emperor. Under his authority, the city of Dhaka and Mughal power in the province attained its greatest heights. In the year 1660, he was assigned as the Mughal Viceroy in the struggle against the Maratha rebel Ch. Shivaji Maharaj he barely survived and grieved the death of a son. He was awarded many honors and gifts by the Mughal Emperor. Mirza Abu Talib is of

Iranian origin. His grandfather and father, Mirza
Ghias Beg Itimaduddaula and Asaf Khan, were
the wazirs (or Prime Ministers) of the Mughal
Emperors Shahjahan and Jahangir respectively.
Emperor Jahangir awarded the title of Shaista Khan
to Mirza in recognition of his family's service and
position in the Mughal court.

Shaista Khan trained and served with the Mughal
army and court, winning multiple promotions and
appointed governor of various provinces. He also
developed a reputation for being a successful
military commander and grew close to the prince
Aurangzeb when the duo fought against the
kingdom of Golconda.

After his accession to the throne and after the
dramatic death of Afzal Khan, Aurangzeb sent
Shaista Khan as viceroy of the Deccan with a large
army to defeat Shivaji. In January, 1660 Shaista
Khan arrived at Aurangabad and quickly
advancing seized Pune, this city was the renown
center of Shivaji's realm. He also captured the fort
of Chakan, Kalyan and north Konkan after heavy
fighting with the Maratha. The Maratha were
banned from entering the city of Pune and Mughal
distance from the locals turned out to be an error.
On April 5, 1663 evening, a wedding party had
obtained special permission for taking out a
procession. Shivaji and many of his nearly 400
men disguised as the bridegroom's procession
members entered Pune. Others entered in small
parties dressed as laborers and soldiers of Maratha
generals serving under Shaista khan. After
midnight, they raided the Nawab's compound and

then entered the palace in an attempt to assassinate the Mughal Viceroy Shaista Khan.

Shaista Khan was clearly unaware, and unprepared The Marathas broke into the courtyard of the palace slaughtered Mughal palace guards. Shaista Khan lost his three fingers in a skirmish with Shivaji, while his son was killed in an encounter with the Marathas in the palace courtyard. Forty attendants and six women were also killed. Taking advantage of confusion and the dark hours, the Marathas escaped the palace and Pune town, despite widespread camping of Mughal forces. Shocked by the sudden and bold attack in Pune, Aurangzeb transferred Shaista Khan back to Bengal and awarded him many honors and gifts for his short lived struggle.

Upon his arrival in Bengal, Shaista Khan was immediately engrossed in putting down the rebellions of hill tribes. Shaista Khan foresaw a potent threat from the Arakan kingdom (in modern Myanmar), which had developed its military and naval strength. He immediately began developing the Mughal navy, increasing its fleet to as many as 300 ships within a year. He also made strenuous diplomatic efforts to win the support of the Dutch East India Company as well as Portugal, which was supporting Arakan with resources and troops. With active Dutch military support, Shaista Khan led Mughal forces on an assault on the island of Sandwip, which lay in Arakanese control. Shaista Khan gained a considerable advantage when a conflict erupted between the Arakanese and the Portuguese. By promptly offering protection and support, Khan sequestered the aid of the Portuguese against the Arakanese and Mughal forces succeeded in capturing the island in November, 1665.

In December 1665 Shaista Khan launched a major military campaign against Chittagong, which was the mainstay of the Arakenese kingdom. The imperial fleet consisted of 288 vessels of their own and about 40 vessels of the Ferinigis (Portuguese) as auxiliaries. Ibn Hussain, Shaista Khan's admiral, was asked to lead the navy, while the subahdar himself took up the responsibility of supplying provisions for the campaign. The overall command was given to Buzurg Ummed Khan, a son of Shaista Khan. The Mughals and the Portuguese held sway in the following naval battle. The conquered territory was placed under direct imperial administration. The name of Chittagong was changed to Islamabad and it became the headquarters of a Mughal faujdar. Khan also re-asserted Mughal control over Cooch Behar and Kamarupa.

Upon his victory against the Arakanese, he ordered the release of thousands of Bengali peasants being held captive by the Arakanese forces. As governor, Shaista Khan encouraged trade with Europe, Southeast Asia and other parts of India. He consolidated his power by signing trade agreements with European powers. Despite his powerful position he remained loyal to Aurangzeb. Often mediating trade disputes and rivalries, Shaista Khan banned the British East India Company from Bengal after the British demanding greater trading rights and hostile military exchanges erupted between Mughal and British forces.

Shaista Khan encouraged the construction of modern townships, public works in the capital of Dhaka, leading to a massive urban and economic expansion. He was a great patron of the arts and encouraged the construction of majestic monuments across the province, including mosques, mausoleums and palaces that represented the finest in Indo-Sarcenic and Mughal architecture. Khan greatly expanded the Lalbagh Fort, the Chowk Bazaar Mosque, the Satgumbad Mosque and the Choto Katra. He also supervised the construction of a majestic mausoleum for his daughter Bibi Pari.

In his late years, Shaista Khan left Dhaka and returned to Delhi. His legacy was the expansion of Dhaka into a regional centre of trade, politics and culture; a thriving and prosperous city from a small township. The Shaista Khan Mosque is a massive standing monument to Shaista Khan, built on his palace grounds. Incorporating unique elements of Bengali and Mughal architecture, it is a major tourist attraction and a valued historical monument protected by the Government of Bangladesh today.]

At the time, Firangoji Narsala was the *killedar* (commander) of fort Chakan, which was defended by 300–350 Maratha soldiers. They were able to withstand the Mughal attack on the fort for one and a half month. The Mughal force was numbering over 21,000. Then, a *burj* (outer wall) was blown up with explosives. This created an opening to the fort allowing hordes of Mughals to breach the exterior portion of the fort. Firangoji, himself led the Maratha counterattack against a larger Mughal army.

Eventually, the fort was lost with the capture of Firangoji, who then was brought before Shaista Khan, who, appreciating his bravery, offered him a *jahagir* (military commission) on the condition that he join the Mughal forces, which Firangoji declined. Admiring his loyalty, Shaista Khan pardoned Firangoji and set him free. Firangoji returned home and Shivaji awarded him a fort named Bhupalgad.

Shaista Khan pressed his advantage of larger, better provisioned and heavily armed Mughal army and made inroads into some of the Maratha territory. Although he held Pune for almost a year, he had little further success. He had set up his residence at Lal Mahal, Shivaji's palace, in the city of Pune.

Shaista Khan kept a tight security in Pune. However, Shivaji planned an attack on Shaista Khan amidst tight security. In April 1663, a wedding party had obtained special permission for a procession; Shivaji planned an attack using the wedding party as cover. The Marathas disguised themselves as the bridegroom's procession and entered Pune. Shivaji, having spent much of his youth in Pune, knew his way around the city and his own palace of Lal Mahal. Chimanaji Deshpande- one of the childhood friends of Shivaji aided him in this attack offering his services as a personal bodyguard.

According to Babasaheb Purandare, since Mughal army also consisted of Maratha soldiers, it was difficult for someone to distinguish between Shivaji's Maratha soldiers and the Maratha soldiers of the Mughal army. Thus, taking advantage of this situation, Shivaji, along with a few of his trusted men, infiltrated the Mughal camp.

After overpowering and slaying of the palace guards, the Marathas broke into the mansion by breaching an outer wall. Chimnaji and Netaji Palkar entered first along with Babaji Deshpande, another of Shivaji's long time loyal associates, they approached Shaista Khan's quarters. Shivaji then personally confronted Shaista Khan in a face to face attack. Meanwhile, perceiving danger, one of Shaista's wives turned off the lights.

Shivaji pursued Shaista Khan and severed three of his fingers with his sword (in the darkness) as he fled through an open window. Shaista Khan narrowly escaped death and lost his son and many of his guards and soldiers in the raid. Within twenty-four hours of this attack, Shaista Khan left Pune and headed north towards Agra. An angered Aurangzeb transferred him to distant Bengal as a punishment for bringing embarrassment to the Mughals with his ignoble defeat in Pune.

□□□

# Chapter 13

# Battle of Surat

Battle of Surat was a land battle that took place on January 5, 1664 near the city of Surat, Gujarat, India between Chhatrapati Shivaji Maharaj and Inayat Khan, a Mughal captain. The Marathas defeated the small Mughal force. The battle is known for strategic movement of cavalry by Shivaji through enemy's terrain covering almost a distance of 300 km.

As Shaista Khan was in Maharashtra for more than three years, the financial condition of the state was dire. So to improve his finances, Shivaji planned to attack Surat, a key Mughal power centre, and a wealthy port town which generated a million rupees in taxes.

## Battle

*Composition of Mughal Forces*

The defences of the city were poor, as the local Subedar, Inayat Khan appointed by Aurangzeb appointed only 1000 men at arms in his service, this error led to the massacre of innocent civilians by the Maratha. After sacking the Mughal garrison Shivaji attacked the port of Surat and set the local shipping industry ablaze.

In January 1664, Shivaji led 4,000 Maratha soldiers to sack the city Surat, the most important Mughal imperial port, home to over 200,000 people. The Mughal Faujdar Inayat Khan and the 5000 soldiers in his command were overrun and fled to the safety of the citadel. the Marathas then sacked the city, and looted the wealth from trading centers and houses belonging to rich merchants such as Baharji Bohra an Ismaili Muslim.

### Composition of Maratha Forces

Shivaji was assisted by notable commanders along with cavalry of 8000 or more.

### Movement and Clash of Forces

When Shivaji arrived at Surat he demanded tribute from the Mughal commander and a small army stationed for port security, which was refused. The Mughal Sardar, not the bravest, was very surprised by the suddenness of the attack and not willing to face the Maratha forces, he hid himself in the fort of Surat. However, there was an attempt of life on Shivaji by the emissary sent by the Mughal sardar. So Shivaji took the city and put it to the sack.

Surat was under sack for nearly 3 days, in which the Maratha army looted all possible wealth from Mughal and Portuguese trading centers. The Maratha soldiers took away cash, gold, silver, pearls, rubies, diamonds and emeralds from the houses of rich merchants such as Virji Vora, Haji Zahid Beg, Haji Kasim and others. The business of Mohandas Parekh, the deceased broker of the Dutch East India Company, was spared as he was reputed as a charitable man. Similarly, Shivaji did not plunder the houses of the foreign missioneries. The French traveller Francois Bernier wrote in his *Travels in Mughal India*:

I forgot to mention that during pillage of Sourate, Seva-ji, the Holy Seva-ji! Respected the habitation of the reverend father Ambrose, the Capuchin missionary. 'The Frankish Padres are good men', he said 'and shall not be attacked.'

The total number of prisoners executed during the raid was 4; the hands of another 24 were cut off. Shivaji had to complete the sacking of Surat before the Mughal Empire at Delhi was alerted and could not afford to waste much time in attacking the British.

Thus, Sir George Oxenden was able to successfully defend the British factory, a fortified warehouse-counting house-hostel.

### Atrocities

One Englishman named Anthony Smith, was captured by the Marathas, he was forced to witness cruel methods of torture inflicted upon prisoners who were ordinary and innocent subjects of the Mughal Empire, Anthony Smith even mentioned how Shivaji's raiders punitively maimed and executed those prisoners by cutting off their hands and heads.

When the Mughal Army finally approached on the fourth fateful day, Shivaji and his bandits galloped southwards into the Deccan.

Only the well organized British led by George Oxenden and the Portuguese survived the onslaught, but the city itself never recovered.

### Outcome

All this loot was successfully transported to Maharashtra before the Mughal Empire at Delhi could get the news of the sacking of Surat. This wealth later was used for developing & strengthening the Maratha Empire.

## Casualties

No casualties with Maratha forces. There were 4 Mughal prisoners killed and hands of 24 prisoners were chopped off after mughal envoy suddenly tried to kill Shivaji with a dagger.

❑❑❑

# Chapter 14

# Battle of Sinhagad

The Battle of Sinhagad was a night battle that took place on February 4, 1670 in the fort of Sinhagad, near the city of Pune, Maharashtra, India. It was fought between Tanaji Malusare, a commander of Maratha ruler Shivaji and Udaybhan Rathod, fortkeeper under Jai Singh I. Tanaji's army won the war to hand over control of the fort to the Marathas with casualties 300 from Mughal side and 50 from Marathas as well as around 4000 Mughal troops imprisoned by mere 500 Marathas.

The fort, which was previously known as Kondana, was controlled by Mirza Raja Jai Singh, and was strategically located amidst other forts in the region such as Rajgad, Purandar and Torna. The Mughals maintained an army of roughly 5000 men led by Udaybhan, a relative of Jai Singh, and the fort itself was defended by cannons at each turret.

Only one turret was left unguarded as it was at the top of a steep cliff, which was thought impossible to scale. Tanaji was able to infiltrate the fort and carry out a surveillance. He also discovered that there was a party on the night of the battle, so the Mughal soldiers would

be off their guard. Tanaji was assisted by his brother
Suryaji along with 300 Mavalas, who were light infantry
of Maval.

Sinhagad, Sinhgarh, or Sinhgad, is a fortress located
roughly 30 kilometres southwest of the city of Pune, India.
Previously called Kondhana, the fort has been the site of
many important battles, most notably the battle of
Sinhagad in 1670. It was also strategically located at the
centre of a string of other forts such as Rajgad, Purandar
and Torna.

Perched on an isolated cliff of the Bhuleswar range
of the Sahyadri Mountains, it is situated on a hill rising
1312 metres above sea level. Given natural protection by
its very steep slopes, the walls and bastions were
constructed at only key places; it has two gates – the
Kalyan Darwaza in the south-east and the Pune Darwaza
in the north-east.

This fort has had quite a long history, It was called
'Kondana' after the sage Kaundinya. The Kaundinyeshwar
temple, the caves and the carvings indicate that this fort
had probably been built two thousand years back. It was
captured from the Koli tribal chieftain, Nag Naik, by
Muhammad bin Tughlaq in 1328 AD.

Shahaji Bhosale, as the commander of Ibrahim Adil
Shah I, was entrusted with the control of the Pune region.
His son Shivaji, however, refused to accept the Adilshahi
and initiated the task of setting up Swarajya. He gained
control of Kondana in 1647 by convincing Siddi Amber,
the Adilshahi Sardar who controlled the fort. Bapuji
Mudgal Deshpande played key role in this activity. In
1649, it had to be handed over to Adil Shah for Shahaji
Maharaj's release. Shivaji Maharaj recaptured it back in

1656 again with the help of Bapuji Mudgal Deshpande, who convinced Fort commander by giving land in newly created Shivapur village and peacefully gained control of fort.This Fort saw attacks of Mughals on 1662, 1663 and 1665. In 1664, Shahistekhan- mughal general even tried to bribe people of fort to hand over the fort to him but he was unsuccessful. Unfortunately in a Purandar Pact it went into the hands of the Mughal army chief Mirzaraje Jaysingh, in the year 1665.

In 1670, Shivaji Maharaj re-conquered this fort and then it stayed under Maratha rule till 1689. After the death of Sambhaji, the Mughals regained control over. Again in 1693 the Marathas recaptured it headed by Sardar Balkawade. Chatrapati Rajaram took asylum on this fort during Mogul raid on Satara but Rajaram died on Sinhagad on the 3rd of March 1700 & in 1703 Aurangzeb conquered the fort. In 1706, it once again went into the hands of the Marathas. Pantaji Shivdev of Sangola and the Pant Pratinidhis played key role in this battle. Then this fort remained with Marathas till 1818, when the British conquered it. British however took three months to capture this fort highest time ever for them to win any fort in the Maharastra.

*Battle of Sinhagad*

One of the most famous battles for Sinhagad was fought to recapture the fort by Tanaji Malusare, a general of Shivaji in March 1670. A steep cliff leading to the fort was scaled with the help of a monitor lizard named yashwanti, colloquially known as a ghorpad. Thereafter, there ensued fierce battles between Tanaji and his men, and the mughal army that had the fort at the time. Tanaji lost his life, but his brother Suryaji took over and captured Kondana.

188 Shivaji and His Campaign

There is an anecdote that upon hearing of Tanaji's death, Shivaji expressed his remorse with the words: "Gad aala pan sinha gela" - "We gained the fort, but lost the lion". The name Sinhagad, though, pre-dates this event, and can be seen in written communiques from the era. Hence, the story that the name was made Sinhagad in honour of Tanaji is true. A bust of Tanaji has been established on the fort in memory of his contribution to the battle. It remains to this day a grand symbol of a great Maratha victory over the invading Muslims.

Pune is well known for its forts and its hilly areas, which attract trek lovers in huge numbers. It has also been one of the eminent tourist spots in the state of Maharashtra. Holding historical structures like Shivneri Fort, Janjira Fort, Sinhagad Fort etc. Pune is also known as the cultural capital of the state. Sinhagad Fort is located to the southwest of Pune at a distance of 25 km. Trekking is the major attraction of the fort.

The fort is also known as Kondhana and forms the centre of all other forts Rajgad, Purandar and Torna surrounding it. The fort is located in the Sahyadri Mountains, on a deserted cliff of Bhuleswar range at a height of 1350m above the sea level.

The walls, the bastions and the slopes of the fort are built with tremendous idea providing natural protection and have been built at only some of the key points. The Fort has only two gates to enter the structure, the Kalyan Darwaza and Pune Darwaza which are positioned at the south east and north-east ends respectively.

Some of the information available at this fort portrays that the fort could have been built 2000 years ago. The caves and the carvings in the Kaundinyeshwar temple stand as proofs for the same. In 1328 AD, Muhammad bin Tughlaq captured the fort from Nag Naik, Koli tribal chief. Since this time, many rulers attempted to capture the fort and it went into the hands in regular intervals. Shivaji, the ruler of Marathas took over the fort in 1647.

Mughals gave a tough fight in capturing the fort, but Marathas never let the fort stay under any one for a long time. The fort was captured by other rulers and recaptured by Marathas at regular intervals, until the British finally captured it in 1818.

The fort is also significant for holding the memorials of Tanaji Malusare and Rajaram, younger son of Shivaji. Tanaji was a general of Shivaji who lost his life in the Battle of Sinhagad. Twentieth Century history reveals that one of the renowned Indian freedom fighter Lokmanya Tilak erected a bungalow above the fort.

Currently the fort serves as a training centre at National Defence Academy, Khadakwasla. And is the picnic spot for the Pune locals and trekking enthusiasts.

### Present Day

Parts of the once extensive fortification are now in ruins, but visitors still sense how the fort acted as an active military outpost. It is a popular weekend destination for many residents of Pune, with some enthusiasts trekking to the top of the fort from the base near Sinhagad village. The site also houses a memorial to Tanaji as well as the tomb of Rajaram, Shivaji's younger son, who also died here. Visitors can see the military stables, brewery and a Kali (godddess) temple along with a Hanuman statue much to the right side of the temple, as well as the historic gates.

The fort is also part of training at National Defence Academy, Khadakwasla. Cadets from the academy are regularly sent on a hikes and runs from NDA to Sinhagad in full battle gear to build endurance and stamina. The fort also houses a television tower for broadcasting local TV signals. Sinhagad is very popular tourist destination today and is frequented by Punekars. There is a steep and narrow two lane road from the base of the fort to the top. The local municipal transport service, the PMPML runs buses every hour from Shanivarwada and Swargate to the Sinhagad foothills. The climbing route from either side of the fort can be covered in around an hour, however it gets slippery in the rainy season. Shared taxi services to the base as well as the top of the mountain are also available.

*Fig.: Sinhagad: View from the "Pune Darwaja"*

## Battle

Legend has it that Tanaji used a monitor lizard named Yeshwanti, with a rope tied around its waist for climbing up the steep vertical rock face. After 342 Maratha reached on the top with Tanaji Malusare, the rope gave away due to abrasion against the rocks and 60 Marathas who were climbing on the rope fell down and died. Tanaji Malusare then instructed his brother Suryaji to continue the attack with other Marathas from the Kalyan darwaja with the assurance that the Mahadeo Kolis would help him get through.

Once inside, they set upon Udaybhan and his men. A fierce combat took place between Tanaji and Udaybhan. Udaybhan managed to rid Tanaji of his shield, who then continued to fight by tying a cloth over one of his hands and using it to ward off Udaybhan's sword attacks. Tanaji fought fiercely in spite of losing his shield. He managed to acquire another sword and was thus fighting Uday Bhan with two swords while the latter fought with a sword and a shield.

At the climax of the battle, each one struck a fatal blow to the other, both collapsing and succumbing to their injuries. The fall of Tanaji created a panic amongst his soldiers who tried to use the ropes as an escape route. Legend states that the ropes were then cut by Tanaji's brother Suryaji forcing the soldiers to either fight or jump down the sheer cliffs to their deaths. This was in line with the ideology of shivaji, wherein the Marathas were not fighting for a king or a master, but for the freedom of their motherland, the Muslims had taken control of.

A loss of the leader should not deter the morale of the force but instead a new leader should take his place without any delay. Tanaji's surprise attack in the dead of the night caught the defenders offguard and the fort was captured by the Marathas. The legend says Shivaji renamed the fort from Kondana to Sinhagad (Lion's Fort) in Tanaji's honor.

## Aftermath

Nearly 1500 Mughal infantry fled to Pune from Sinhagad after the battle taking advantage of darkness of midnight. This battle significantly boosted confidence of Marathas and within two months after this battle Marathas won all nearby forts like Purandar, Lohagad so on. Till beginning of rainy monsoon season, excluding Pune, Indapur and Baramati all regions were won by Marathas. In June 1670, the Mogul army was totally unprepared and ill-equipped as monsoon had arrived. Sensing this as unique opportunity Chatrapati Shivaji decided to attack urban area of Pune, Baramati, Supe and Indapur in the rainy season. Within 10–15 days, Marathas captured all these areas from Mughal Empire, this transition happened nearly after 10 years that is in 1660, these cities were captured by Mughal army headed by Shahista Khan.

## Legacy

Upon hearing the news of the capture of the fort at the cost of Tanaji's life, Shivaji was greatly aggrieved and is said to have remarked, "Gad aala, pan sinha gela" - "We captured the fort but lost the lion". The fort was renamed from Kondana to Sinhagad, in honor of Tanaji.

Today, there is a monument with a bust of Tanaji in honor of his valour. The name of the road from Pune City to Fort is known as Tanaji Malusare Road.

□□□

# Chapter 15

# Maratha War of Independence

The Maratha War of Independence (also termed the War of 27 years) was fought between the Maratha Empire and the Mughal Empire from 1681 to 1707 on the Indian subcontinent. It is the longest recorded military engagement in the history of India. It started in 1681 with the Mughal emperor Aurangzeb's invasion of the Maratha Empire. Despite the Mughal army's vast numerical superiority, the empire's treasury, and the support of allies such as the Portuguese, British, Siddhis, Golkonda and Bijapur sultanates, the war ended in 1707 with a victory for the Maratha empire.

*Fig.: Shivaji was the founder of the Maratha Empire. Statue of Shivaji at Raigad Fort*

Emperor (*Chhatrapati*) Shivaji, the founder of the Maratha Empire, died in 1680. At that time, the Marathas had emerged as the dominant power in peninsular India. Prior to his death, Shivaji had conquered the Deccan and emerged as the sole power to challenge the Mughal's southward expansion into southern India. The Bijapur Sultanate under Sikandar Adil Shah, an ally of Shivaji, was in decline. The Hyderabad Sultanate was also allied with Shivaji.

Soon after Shivaji's death, the Mughal Emporer (*Badshah*) Aurangzeb decided to personally lead his army against the Marathas to reclaim the lost territory in the Deccan. The War of 27 years started in 1681.

The war can be broken down into three distinct phases:

1) Marathas under Sambhaji (1681–1689): Concluding with the fall of Raigad Fort and the execution of Sambhaji.

2) Marathas under Rajaram (1689–1699): Concluding with the fall of Jinji and the death of Rajaram.

3) Victory of Marathas under Tarabai (1699–1707): Concluding with victory of the Maratha Empire under Tarabai and the death of Aurangzeb.

## Marathas under Sambhaji (1681-1689)

In the first half of 1681, many Mughal contingents were dispatched to lay siege to Maratha forts in present day Gujarat, Maharashtra, Karnataka, and Madhya Pradesh. In September of 1681, after settling his dispute with the royal house of Mewar, Aurangzeb began his journey to Deccan to kill the Maratha confederacy that was not too old. He arrived at Aurangabad, the Mughal headquarters in the Deccan and made it his capital.

Mughal contingents in the region numbered about 500,000. It was a disproportionate battle in all senses. By the end of 1681, the Mughal forces had laid siege to Fort Ramsej. But the Marathas did not succumb to this onslaught. The attack was well received and it took the Mughals seven years to win the fort. In December 1681, Sambhaji attacked Janjira, but his first attempt failed. In the same time one of the Aurangzeb's generals, Husain Ali Khan, attacked Northern Konkan. Sambhaji left janjira and attacked Husain Ali Khan and pushed him back to Ahmednagar. Aurangzeb tried to sign a deal with Portuguese to allow trade ships to harbor in Goa. This would have allowed him to open another supply route to Deccan via sea.

The news reached sambhaji. He attacked Portuguese territories and pushed them deep inside Goa. But Viceroy of Alvor was able to defend Portughese headquarters. By this time massive Mughal army had started gathering on the borders of Deccan. It was clear that southern India was headed for one big conflict.

In late 1683, Aurangzeb moved to Ahmednagar. He divided his forces in two and put his two princes, Shah Alam and Azam Shah, in charge of each division. Shah Alam was to attack South Konkan via Karnataka border while Azam Shah would attack Khandesh and northern Maratha territory. Using pincer strategy, these two divisions planned to circle Marathas from South and North and isolate them.

The beginning went quite well. Shah Alam crossed Krishna River and enterd Belgaum. From there he entered Goa and started marching north via Konkan. As he pushed further, he was continuously harassed by Marathas. They ransacked his supply chains and reduced his forces to starvation. Finally Aurangzeb sent Ruhulla Khan for his rescue and brought him back to Ahmednagar. The first pincer attempt failed.

After 1684 monsoon, Aurangzeb's another general Shahbuddin Khan directly attacked the Maratha capital, Raigad. Maratha commanders successfully defended Raigad. Aurangzeb sent Khan Jehan for help, but Hambirao Mohite, commander-in-chief of Maratha army, defeated him in a fierce battle at Patadi. Second division of Maratha army attacked Shahbuddin Khan at Pachad, inflicting heavy losses on Mughal army.

In early 1685, Shah Alam attacked South again via Gokak-Dharwar route. But Sambhaji's forces harassed him continuously on the way and finally he had to give up and thus failed to close the loop second time. In April 1685, Aurangzeb rehashed his strategy. He planned to consolidate his power in the South by taking expeditions to the Muslim kingdoms Golkonda and Bijapur. Both of them were allies of Marathas and Aurangzeb was not fond of them. He broke his treaties with both kingdoms, attacked them and captured them by September 1686.

Taking this opportunity, Marathas launched an offensive on the North coast and attacked Bharuch. They were able to evade the Mughal army sent their way and came back with minimum damage. Marathas tried to win Mysore through diplomacy. *Sardar* Kesopant Pingle was running negotiations, but the fall of Bijapur to the Mughals turned the tides and Mysore was reluctant to join Marathas.

Sambhaji successfully courted several Bijapur *sardars* to join the Maratha army. Sambhaji led the fight valiantly but was treacherously captured by the Mughals and killed. His wife and son (Shivaji's grandson) were held captive by Aurangzeb for twenty years.

*Execution of Sambhaji*

*Fig.: Stone arch at Tulapur confluence where Sambhaji was executed.*

After fall of Bijapur and Goalkonda, Aurangzeb turned his attention again to his main target – Marathas. First few attempts proved unsuccessful to make a major dent. In Jan 1688, Sambhaji called his commanders for a strategic meeting at Sangameshwar in Konkan to decide on the final blow to oust Aurangzeb from Deccan. In order to execute the plans soon, Sambhaji sent ahead most of his comrades and stayed back with a few of his trustworthy men.

Ganoji Shirke, one of Sambhaji's brother-in-laws, turned a traitor and helped Aurangzeb's commander Muqarrab Khan to locate, reach and attack Sangameshwar when Sambhaji was in the garden of Sangameshwar, resolving some issues and was about to leave the town. Sambhaji, Kavi Kalash and his men were surrounded from all sides. Marathas took out their swords, roared 'Har Har Mahadev' and pounced upon the far too numerous Mughals. A bloody skirmish took place and Sambhaji was captured on 1 February 1689. Maratha soldiers and other faithfuls unsuccessfully tried to rescue Sambhaji but were killed by Mughals on 3 February 1689.

Sambhaji was beheaded and his body was cut into pieces on his denial to bow down to Aurangzeb and convert to Islam.

[Muqarrab Khan of Golconda (titled Khan-Zaman Fath Jang) was the most experienced commander in Golconda, during the reign of Abul Hasan Qutb Shah. Muqarrab Khan is known to have been an ally of Afzal Khan and defended Golcondas southern realms against Maratha raids. Muqarrab Khan was a political rival of Abul Hasan Qutb Shah's cruel Brahman viziers Madanna and Akkanna.

After Abul Hasan Qutb Shah, escaped from his administrative duties by retreating into the Golconda Fort along with 1000 women who were known for their mastery in music and song. Muqarrab Khan had become the *de facto* ruler of Golconda.

Before, Aurangzeb and his forces initiated the Siege of Golconda, Muqarrab Khan the most experienced commander in Golconda, defected to the Mughals. Muqarrab Khan and his forces proved their fighting experience and worth against the Maratha when he led a contingent that eventually hunted down Sambhaji at Sangameshwar and brought him to justice (for the slaughtering of innocent people).

Sambhaji and his men were captured by Muqarrab Khan and his Mughal contingent of 25,000. When Sambhaji was presented before the Mughal Emperor Aurangzeb, he the emperor knelt in prayer and thanksgiving to Allah. When Sambhaji, was questioned for the atrocities he had committed, he responded with insults to the Mughal Emperor Aurangzeb, which were tolerated, but he sealed his fate by insulting the Prophet Muhammad. A panel of Qadi's of the Mughal Empire indited and sentenced Sambhaji to death for slaying innocent people, for condoning casual rape, torture, arson, looting and massacre of good Muslims particularly for the atrocities committed during his ravaging of Burhanpurand its populace.]

## Marathas under King Rajaram (1689 to 1700)

To Aurangzeb, the Marathas seemed all but dead by end of 1689. But this would prove to be almost a fatal blunder. The death of Sambhaji had rekindled the spirit of the Maratha forces, which made Aurangzeb's mission impossible. Sambhaji's younger brother Rajaram was now given the title of 'Chhatrapati' (king). In March 1690, the Maratha commanders, under the leadership of Santaji Ghorpade launched the single most daring attack on mughal army.

They not only attacked the army, but sacked the tent where the Aurangzeb himself slept. Luckily Aurangzeb was elsewhere but his private force and many of his bodyguards were killed. This brought disgrace to the Mughals. This positive development was followed by a negative one for Marathas. Raigad fell to treachery of Suryaji Pisal. Sambhaji's queen, Yesubai and their son, Shahu, were captured.

Mughal forces, led by Zulfikar Khan, continued this offensive further South. They attacked fort Panhala. The Maratha killedar of Panhala gallantly defended the fort and inflicted heavy losses on Mughal army. Finally Aurangzeb himself had to come. Panhala surrendered.

*Shift of Maratha Capital to Jinji*

Maratha ministers had foreseen the next Mughal move on Vishalgad. They insisted Rajaram to leave Vishalgad for Jinji (in present Tamil Nadu), was earlier captured by Shivaji during his southern conquests. Rajaram travelled South under escort of Khando Ballal and his men. Jinji became new capital of Marathas. This breathed new life in Maratha army. It was to be the Maratha capital for next seven years.

Aurangzeb was frustrated with Rajaram's successful escape. His next move was to keep most of his force in Maharashtra and dispatch a small force to keep Rajaram in check. But the two Maratha generals, Santaji Ghorpade and Dhanaji Jadhav would prove more than match to him. They first attacked and destroyed the force sent by Aurangzeb to keep check on Rajaram, thus relieving the immediate danger. Then they joined Ramchandra Bavadekar in Deccan. Bavdekar, Vithoji chavan and Raghuji Bhosale had reorganized most of the Maratha army after defeats at Panhala and Vishalgad.

In late 1691, Bavdekar, Pralhad Niraji, Santaji, Dhanaji and several Maratha sardars met in Maval region and reformed the strategy. Aurangzeb had taken four major forts in Sahyadrais and was sending Zulfikar khan to subdue the fort Jinji. So according to new Maratha plan, Santaji and Dhanaji would launch offensives in the East to keep rest of the Mughal forces scattered. Others would focus in Maharashtra and would attack a series of forts around Southern Maharashtra and Northern Karnataka to divide Mughal won territories in two, thereby posing significant challenge to enemy supply chains. Having a strong navy established by Shivaji, Marathas could now extend this divide into the sea, checking any supply routes from Surat to South.

Now war was fought from the Malwa plateau to the east coast. Such was the strategy of Maratha commanders to counter the might of the Mughals. Maratha generals Ramchandrapant Amatya and Shankaraji Niraji maintained the Maratha stronghold in the rugged terrains of Sahyadri.

In several brilliant cavalry movements, Santaji Ghorpade and Dhanaji Jadhav defeated the Mughals. Their offensive, and especially that of Santaji, struck terror into the hearts of the Mughals. In the Battle of Athani, Santaji defeated Kasim Khan, a noted Mughal general.

## Fall of Jinji (Jan 1698)

By now, Aurangzeb had the grim realization that the war he began was much more serious than he thought. He consolidated his forces and rethought his strategy. He sent an ultimatum to Zulfikar khan to finish Jinji business or be stripped of the titles. Zulfikar Khan tightened the Siege. But Rajaram escaped and was safely escorted to Deccan by Dhanaji Jadhav and Shirke brothers.

Haraji Mahadik's son took the charge of Jinji and bravely defended Jinji against Julfikar khan and Daud khan till January of 1698. This gave Rajaram ample of time to reach Vishalgad. After great loses, Jinji was captured but it did a big damage to the Mughal Empire. The losses incurred in taking Jinji far outweighed the gains. The fort had done its work.

For seven years the three hills of Jinji had kept a large contigent of Mughal forces occupied. It had eaten a deep hole into Mughal resources. Not only at Jinji, but the royal treasury was bleeding everywhere and was already under strain.

Marathas would soon witness an unpleasant development, all of their own making. Dhanaji Jadhav and Santaji Ghorpade had a simmering rivalry, which was kept in check by the councilman Pralhad Niraji. But after Niraji's death, Dhanaji grew bold and attacked Santaji. Nagoji Mane, one of Dhanaji's men, killed Santaji. The news of Santaji's death greatly encouraged Aurangzeb and Mughal army.

But by this time Mughals were no longer the army they were feared before. Aurangzeb, against advise of several of his experienced generals, kept the war on. The situation was much like Alexander on the borders of Taxila.

The Siege of Jinji, (September, 1690–January 8, 1698), began when the Mughal Emperor Aurangzeb appointed Zulfiqar Ali Khan as the Nawab of the Carnatic and dispatched him to besiege and capture Jinji Fort, which had been sacked and captured by Marathas led by Rajaram, they had also ambushed and killed about 300 Mughal Sowars in the Carnatic. TheMughal Emperor Aurangzeb then ordered Ghazi ud-Din Khan Feroze Jung I to protect the supply routes leading to Jinji Fortand to support and provide reinforcements to Zulfiqar Ali Khan when needed.

The Siege of Jinji, was also the longest siege by any single Mughal Army in recorded history, it lasted for a lingering 8 years. Jinji Fort itself was under the control of the Adil Shahis of Bijapur since the year 1649. Until in the year 1677, Sivaji, routed the Bijapur forces and captured Jinji Fort. The fort itself was chosen as a hideout for the renegade Maratha leader Rajaramand his allies Santaji Ghorpade and Dhanaji Jadhav.

Outraged by the deaths of the Mughal Sowars in the region the Mughal Emperor Aurangzeb dispatched Zulfiqar Ali Khan to besiege and capture the massive Jinji Fort.

But besieging the fort was no easy task. It enclosed an area of 7 sq km (2.7 sq mi), and its walls were 30ft high and 66ft thick. It is elevated 800ft (240 m) high, and protected by a 80 feet (24 m) wide moat. There were three very important hills within the fort and a large pond containing fresh water. Immediately after encircling the fort in the year 1690, with his Mughal Sowars and Zamburak, Zulfiqar Ali Khan placed Swarup Singh and young Mehboob Khan (a Tamil Muslim nicknamed *Maavuthukaran*) in command of the Sepoys. Daud Khan was appointed *Mir Atish* or lead gunner of 60 cannon placed at various locations. Fatah Muhammad was the lead commander of the Rocket artillery consisting of 50 men. Muslim Mappila and Tamils were recruited and good relations were established with Ali Raja Ali II.

Zulfiqar Ali Khan then ordered the Maratha to surrender but Rajaram refused and the bombardments began but with little success. Desperately searching for a quick victory Zulfiqar Ali Khan made all efforts to gather men, ammunition and money for a successful war with them. He even allied himself with Fort St. George's English Governor Elihu Yale.

In the coming years Zulfiqar Ali Khan would attempt to breach the walls with limited resources he managed to protect the trade routes and make contact with Ghazi ud-Din Khan Feroze Jung I on many occasions. He defended nearby land owners, and led four massive assaults upon the Marathas inside the fort. However, most of his focus was towards the vicinity of the fort and he continuously expected and correctly predicted Maratha ambushes instead of besieging the fort itself.

Zulfikhar Ali Khan was briefly joined by Aurangzeb's son Prince Muhammad Kam Baksh. On one occasion when the Mughal encampments around Jinji fort were surrounded by the Maratha rebels, actually decided to defect his plans were foiled and was put to chains and imprisoned in a ditch which was covered by a tent by Zulfikhar Ali Khan, who managed to expel the roving Marathas with Matchlocks. Zulfikhar Ali Khan then wrote a letter informing the Mughal Emperor of his son's betrayal, Aurangzeb then sent his trusted vizier Asad Khan to retrieve Prince Muhammad Kam Baksh. Asad Khan arrived with the finest weapons, carriages and thousands of reinforcements. When Prince Muhammad Kam Baksh, was brought in chains before Aurangzeb, the Mughal Emperor almost had him beheaded, but Aurangzeb was deterred by the pleas of his own daughter Zinat-un-nissa.

Queen Mangammal had realized that the renegade Rajaram had entrenched himself within Jinji and had been bent upon attacking Thanjavur and Madurai if the Mughal Army was to withdraw. Mangammal soon recognized Aurangzeb as her suzerain and began to assist Zulfikhar Ali Khan.

Zulfikhar Ali Khan then setup a base in Wandiwash, in the year 1697 Zulfikhar Ali Khan led 18,000 men from his camp (8000 Sowars and 10,000 Sepoys) in order to fight an assembling Maratha force in Tanjore sent by Shivaji II and Ramchandra Pant Amatya and possibly aided by the Madurai Nayaks, consisting of over 40,000men with the objective to relieve the siege of Jinji

Fort and continue their hostilities against the Mughal Empire. Zulfikhar Ali Khan and his considerably smaller battalion then defeated the ill-equipped Maratha and routed them.

Because Zulfikhar Ali Khan did not often receive assistance and supplies from the Mughals he began to forage the countryside in order to recover his losses. In 1697 Rajaram offered to negotiate, but Aurangzeb ordered Zulfikhar Ali Khan to initiate an all-out assault. Zulfikhar Ali Khan returned he made efforts to hire European gunners and then led his final fourth assault into Jinji Fort in the year 1698. Forced into action the Mughal Army battered the walls with cannon-fire, which eventually allowed them to scale the walls and capture the lower citadels, which were armed with cannons that bombarded the higher citadel. After heavy bombardments the Mughals captured the higher citadel. Zulfikhar Ali Khan captured four of Rajaram's wives, three sons and two daughters, while Rajaram himself fled.

According to Mughal accounts Zulfikhar Ali Khan named Jinji Fort, "Nusratgarh" after its capture, but the condemned Maratha leader Rajaram had somehow escaped earlier on during the siege, causing much dismay for Zulfikhar Ali Khan. However, the Mughal rule at Jinji eventually led to the establishment of the Nawab of the Carnatic and the Sultanate of Mysore.

But according to Hindu accounts: it was due to the efforts of Swarup Singh of Bundela, that the Mughals were successful, the Mughal Emperor Aurangazeb, himself granted Swarup Singh a position of Mansabdar of 2,500 and gave him total command and administration of Jinji Fort in 1700 AD. But after Sawrup Singh died of old age in 1714, his newly arriving son De Singh was given command according to an official Firman by the Mughal Emperor Jahandar Shah. This action was considered outrageous to Muhammed Saadatullah Khan Iwho personally marched to Jinji Fort with 18,000 men and killed De Singh and declared himself the administrator of Jinji Fort.

## Revival of Strong Maratha Position

The Marathas again consolidated and the new Maratha counter offensive began. Rajaram made Dhanaji the next commander in chief. Maratha army was divided in three divisions. Dhanaji would himself lead the first division. Parshuram Timbak led the second and Shankar Narayan led the third. Dhanaji Jadhav defeated a large mughal force near Pandharpur. Shankar Narayan defeated Sarja Khan in Pune.

Khanderao Dabhade, who led a division under Dhanaji, took Baglan and Nashik. Nemaji Shinde, another commander with Shankar Narayan, scored a major victory at Nandurbar. Enraged at this defeat, Aurangzeb himself took charge and launched another counter offensive. He laid siege to Panhala and attacked the fort of Satara. The seasoned commander, Prayagji Prabhu defended Satara for a good six months, but surrendered in April of 1700, just before onset of Monsoon. This foiled Aurangzeb's strategy to clear as many forts before monsoon as possible.

## Victory of Marathas under Tarabai (1700-1707)

In March of 1700, Rajaram took his last breath. His queen Tarabai, who was also daughter of the gallant Maratha Commander-in-Chief Hambirao Mohite, took charge of Maratha army. Daughter of a braveheart, Tarabai proved her true mettle for the next seven years. She carried the struggle on with equal valor. Thus began the phase III, the last phase of the prolonged war, with Marathas under the leadership of Tarabai.

[Tarabai (1675–1761 CE) was a queen of the Maratha Empire in India. Her husband was Chhatrapati Rajaram, son of Shivaji. Tarabai was the daughter of the famed Maratha generalHambirao Mohite. She was the niece of Soyarabai, the second wife Chatrapati Shivaji.

Tarabai was skilled in cavalry movement, and made strategic movements herself during wars. She personally led the war and continued the insurgency against the Mughals. A trucewas offered to the Mughals in such way that it was promptly rejected by the Mughal emperor, and Tarabai continued the Maratha resistance.

By 1705, Marathas had crossed the Narmada and made small incursions in Malwa, retreating immediately. The Maratha country was relieved at the news of the death of Mughal emperor Aurangzeb who died at Khuldabad in Aurangabad.

In order to divide the Maratha onslaught, the Mughals released Shahu on certain conditions. He immediately challenged Tarabai and Shivaji II for leadership of the Maratha polity. Shahu eventually prevailed thanks to his legal position and in part to the Peshwa Balaji Vishwanath' diplomacy, and Tarabai was sidelined for some time. She established a rival court in Kolhapur in 1713.

After Shahu's death in 1749, Tarabai helped conduct Ramaraja to the kingship. Afterward, however, she denounced Ramaraja on the grounds that he was not her grandson as he claimed. During this period of weakened royal power, Tarabai exercised great influence in the Maratha state. She headed one of several factions vying for control within the increasingly fractious confederacy.

Hailed as Bhadrakali, her name is still celebrated in countryside in parts of Maharashtra. Noted historian Jadunath Sarkar has written about her, "In that awful crisis her character and strength saved the nation".]

[Hambirao Mohite was *Sardar Senapati* (Commander-in-Chief, Duke) of the Maratha Empire and the brother of Soyarabai, Shivaji's Queen. He was the father of Tarabai, the first regent of Kolhapur. Following Emperor Shivaji's death in 1680, as *Senapati*, he played an important role backing Sambhaji (his eldest nephew) in his claim to the throne of the Maratha empire and in his battles against Aurangzeb.

An able general and brave soldier, he fiercely resisted the half million-strong Mughal army with only a fraction of that under his command. He died a soldier's death after being struck by a cannonball during a battle near Wai in Satara.

Hamirrao Mohite, actually named Hansajirao Mohite, was Conferred title of Hambirrao by Chhatrapati Shivaji. While his ancestors conferred title *Baji* and Deshmukh rights by Deccan Sultanates. He was succeeded by four sons and a daughter namely Santaji, Ranasing, Rangoji, Chandoji and Tarabai (Later rendered Queen Chhatrapati Tarabai Rajaram Bhosale).]

After death of Rajaram, his widow, Tarabai assumed the charge of the empire. She herself took to the field and remained mobile and vigil during the crisis. In words of Jadunath Sarkar, 'It is her character that saved the nation in that awful crisis.'

The signs of strains were showing in Mughal camp in late 1701. Asad Khan, Julfikar Khan's father, counselled Aurangzeb to end the war and turn around. This expedition had already taken a giant toll, much larger than originally planned, on Mughal Empire. And serious signs were emerging that the 200 years old Mughal Empire was crumbling and was in the middle of a war that was not winnable.

Mughals were bleeding heavily from treasuries. But Aurangzeb kept pressing the war on. By 1704, Aurangzeb had Torana and Rajgad. He had won only a handful fort in this offensive, but he had spent several precious years. It was slowly dawning to him that after 24 years of constant war, he was no closer to defeating Marathas than he was the day he began.

The final Maratha counter offensive gathered momentum in North. Tarabai proved to be a valiant leader once again. One after another Mughal provinces fell in north. They were not in position to defend as the royal treasuries had been sucked dry and no armies were left in town. In 1705, two Maratha army factions crossed Narmada. One under leadership of Nemaji Shinde hit as deep North as Bhopal.

Second under the leadership of Dabhade struck Bharoch and West. Dabhade with his eight thousand men, attacked and defeated Mahomed khan's forces numbering almost fourteen thousand. This left entire Gujarat coast wide open for Marathas. They immediately tightened their grip on Mughal supply chains. By 1705 end, Marathas had penetrated Mughal possession of Central India and Gujarat. Nemaji Shinde defeated Mughals on the Malwa plateau. In 1706, Mughals started retreating from Maratha dominions.

In Maharashtra, Aurangzeb grew despondent. He started negotiations with Marathas, but cut abruptly and marched on a small kingdom called Wakinara. Naiks at Wakinara traced their lineage to royal family of Vijaynagar Empire. They were never fond of Mughals and had sided with Marathas. Dhanaji marched into Sahyadris and won almost all the major forts back in short time. Satara and Parali forts were taken by Parshuram Timbak.

Shankar Narayan took Sinhgad. Dhanaji then turned around and took his forces to Wakinara. He helped the Naiks at Wakinara sustain the fight. Naiks fought very bravely. Finally Wakinara fell, but the royal family of Naiks successfully escaped with least damage.

## Aurangzeb's Escape and Death

Aurangzeb had now given up all hopes and was now planning retreat to Burhanpur. Dhanaji Jadhav again fell on him and in swift and ferocious attack and dismantled the rear guard of his imperial army. With the help of Zulfikar Khan, Aurangzeb escaped to Burhanpur.

Aurangzeb witnessed bitter fights among his sons in his last days. Alone, lost, depressed, bankrupt, far away from home, he died on 3 March 1707. "I hope god will forgive me one day for my disastrous sins", were his last words. Thus ended a prolonged and grueling period in history of India. The Mughal kingdom fragmented and disintegrated soon after, paving the way for the Maratha Empire to become the dominant power in India.

## Aftermath of the War

Marathas emerged victorious against the Mughals and started northward expansion. For the first time they crossed the Narmada the traditional boundary between northern plains and peninsula. After defeating the Mughals, there was no other power to oppose Marathas successfully. With the death of Emperor Aurangzeb in 1707, the Maratha army marched in to Delhi itself, within a decade forced the Mughal clan to being confined to Delhi. Under the pressure of Marathas, the Mughals released the grandson of Shivaji, Shahu from captivity.

The Mughals suffered heavy losses in the entire war. Entire Mughal Empire got split in small kingdoms. Nizam of Hyderabad, Nawab of Oudh and Nawab of Bengal quickly declared their kingdoms as independent from Mughal Empire. The Mughals were now confined to Delhi and nearby areas.

Meanwhile the Maratha cavalry continued their expansion in north under various Maratha generals like Nemaji Shinde, Hybtarao Nimbalkar, Parsoji Bhosle, Dhanaji Jadhav and by May 1758, Marathas had extended their territory to Peshawar (now in Pakistan).

❑❑❑

# Chapter 16

# Treaty of Purandar (1665)

The Treaty of Purandar was signed on June 11, 1665, between the Rajput ruler Jai Singh I, who was commander of the Mughal Empire, and Maratha Chhatrapati Shivaji Maharaj. Shivaji was forced to sign the agreement after Jai Singh besieged Purandar fort. When Shivaji realised that war with the Mughal Empire would only cause damage to the empire and that his men would suffer heavy losses, he chose to make a treaty instead of leaving his men under the Mughals.

The veteran general, Jaisingh was not Shashta khan. He did not underestimated Shivaji. His plan was to carry out swift & short campaign against Shivaji. His campaign was brilliantly conceived & equally brilliantly executed. His efforts at isolating Shivaji proved successful. The small chiefs, like Ramnagar & Jawhar, survice hungry officers of Vijapur, flocked to the standard of Vijapur. Siddis of Janjira prompty joined Mughals.

Arriving in Poona, Jaisingh marched towards the fort of Purandar. Ihtishan khan & later Qutub khan were posted at Poona with a force of 4000 horses. Jaisingh left Poona on 14th march 1665. On 29th he reached Saswad.

Diler khan, next in command, had already gone ahead with the troops & strong artillery. Siege of Purandar began on 30th march 1665. Inspite of strong Maratha attacks Mughals succeeded in establishing themselves between the forts of Purandar & Rudramal / Vajragad. The Marathas put up a tough fight.

Same time Netaji Palkar raided Paranda region. *"They made sudden raids & carried out night attacks. They used to block roads & hold inaccessible passes. They also use to set fires to the jungles. Owing to these activities the condition of army of Islam was rendered difficult. A considerable number of animals belonging to the army perished."* In reply Daudkhan was appointed as governor of Khandesh by Jaisingh with 7000 cavalry force. They soon started attacking villages. Setting up fires, capturing men, women & cattle became the set practice of Mughal raiding – parties.

The siege of Purandar is one of the memorable sieges in history of India. Time & again the Marathas emerged from the fort to fall upon Mughal trenches. Hand to hand fights were orders of the day. In such one of the fights, Murar Baji, the gallant Maratha commandant of Purandar, laid down his life. He has become immortal in the Maratha history. Sooner Mughals captured Rudramal on 14th apl. Mughal trenches were moved to the north-east of the fort. They took possession of 5 towers of the forts. Marathas with drew to the inner walls of the fort.

At end of May 1665, Shivaji thought of ending war which was proving ruinous to the country. He approached Jaisingh through more than one latter, offering his cooperation in case of a future Mughal – Vijapur conflict. But the offer was summarily rejected. Jaisingh wanted nothing short of total surrender. Shivaji tried to influence Jaisingh to turn towards Vijapur, so that he could get liberal terms. But Jaisingh refused. Vijapur did make offer to Shivaji to join in hands, but it came to late.

Following are the main points of the treaty:

1. Shivaji kept twelve forts, along with an area worth an income of 1 lakh huns.

2. Shivaji was required to help the Mughals whenever and wherever required.

3. Shivaji's son Sambhaji was tasked with the command of a 5,000-strong force under the Mughals.

4. If Shivaji wanted to claim the Konkan area under Vijapur's control, he would have to pay 40 lakh huns to the Mughals.

5. He had to give up his forts at Purandar, Rudramal, Kondhana, Khandagla, Lohagad, Isagad, Tung, Tikona, Rohida, Nardurga, Mahuli, Bhandardurga, Palaskhol, Rupgad, Bakhtgad, Morabkhan, Manikgad, Saroopgad, Sakargad, Marakgad, Ankola, Songad, and Maangad.

Along with these requirements, Shivaji agreed to visit Agra to meet Aurangzeb for further political talks.

The forts taken away by Mughals were included strong forts like *Lohagad, Visapur, Purandar, Kondana, Rohida, Mahuli*. Only *Rajgad & Torna* of deemed importance was left with Shivaji. The plains of Poona & coastal belt of Kalyan-Bhiwandi were occupied by Mughals. The Mughals extended their sway by taking Siddis in their service. It speaks for the greatness of Shivaji that he bore this humiliation with tremendous forbearance & fortitude. He survived to fight, & fight successfully.

Shivaji took leave Jaisingh in Jan 1666. He was to attack the kingdom of Vijapur from the west & capture Panhala. This was assignment given to him by Jaisingh.

On other hand Diler khan wished to kill Shivaji several times & hence rajah Jaisingh leaved Shivaji for a separate assignment of Panhala. He never listened to the words of Dilerkhan.

On 16th June Shivaji reached Panhala base & led assault. His general Netaji Palkar, did not made it in time. The assault failed with loss of 1000 men. Shivaji got angry on Netaji & withdrew him from post of general. Netaji Palkar sooner left Maratha forces & joined Vijapur & finally joined hands with Mughals with offer of bigger Mansab. Netaji's defection illustrates how even officers nearest to Shivaji failed to understand the significance of the struggle which he was waging.

Vijapur campaign ended disastrously for Jaisingh without sufficient artillery. Sooner Jaisingh feared that Shivaji might join in hands with Vijapur to recapture his forts & territory. It was Jaisingh who suggested Aurangzeb that Shivaji should be called to the court. His letter to Aurangzeb illustrates this simply," *Now that Adilshah & Qutub Shah have united in mischiefs, it is necessary to win Shivaji's heart by all means & send him to northern India to have audience of your majesty."* Jaisingh must have used all his skills in persuading Shivaji to go to Agra he could not hold out any prospects of territorial benefits. Shivaji could not avoid going to the court.

□□□

# Chapter 17

## Ashta Pradhan

The Ashta Pradhan (also termed Asta Pradhad or the Council of 8) was a council of eight ministers that administered the Maratha empire. The council was formed in 1674 by founding Emperor Chhatrapati Shivaji.

The term *Ashta Pradhan* literally translates to "the Prime Eight", from the Sanskrit *ashta* ("eight") and *pradhan* ("prime"). The body discharged the functions of a modern council of ministers; this is regarded as one of the first successful instances of ministerial delegation in India. The council is credited with having implemented good governance practices in the Maratha heartland, as well as for the success of the military campaigns against the Mughal Empire.

### Constitution

The coronation of Shivaji was held in 1674, at the fort of Raigad in present-day Indian state of Maharashtra. On that occasion, Shivaji formalized the institution of a council of eight ministers to guide the administration of his nascent state. This council came to be known as the *Ashta Pradhan*. Each of the ministers was placed in charge of an administrative department; thus, the council heralded the birth of a bureaucracy. The formalization of an administrative mechanism was of a piece with other measures, indicative of the formalization of a sovereign state, which were implemented on the occasion of Shivaji's coronation: coinage bearing Shivaji's insignia (the copper *Shivrai* and the gold *hon*) were issued, and a new era, the *Rajyabhishek era,* was proclaimed on the occasion.

## Composition

Shivaji was an able administrator who established a government that included modern concepts such as cabinet (*Ashtapradhan mandal*),foreign affairs (*Dabir*) and internal intelligence. Shivaji established an effective civil and military administration. He also built a powerful navy. Maynak Bhandari was one of the first chiefs of the Maratha Navy under Shivaji, and helped in both building the Maratha Navy and safeguarding the coastline of the emerging Maratha Empire. He built new forts like Sindhudurg and strengthened old ones like Vijaydurg on the west coast. The Maratha navy held its own against the British, Portuguese and Dutch.

Shivaji is well known for his benevolent attitude towards his subjects. He believed that there was a close bond between the state and the citizens. He encouraged all accomplished and competent individuals to participate in the ongoing political/military struggle. He is remembered as a just and welfare-minded king. He brought revolutionary changes in military organisation, fort architecture, society and politics.

Shivaji was the first king of the medieval world to undertake the revolutionary idea of abolishing the feudal system, 150 years before its worldwide recognition in the French revolution. For a span of about 50 years, there were no feudals in his kingdom. After the fall of Raigadin 1689, Raja Ram started giving land grants to maratha chieftans to fight against the Mughals in the War of 27 years.

The *Ashta Pradhan* was designed to encompass all the primary administrative functions of the state, with each minister being given charge of one role in the administration. Ministerial designations were drawn from the Sanskrit language; the eight ministerial roles were as follows:

*Pantpradhan* or *Peshwa* - Prime Minister, general administration of the Empire.

*Amatya* - Finance Minister, managing accounts of the Empire.

*Sacheev* - Secretary, preparing royal edicts.

*Mantri* - Interior Minister, managing internal affairs.

*Senapati* - Commander-in-Chief, managing the forces and defense of the Empire.

*Sumant* - Foreign Minister, to manage relationships with other sovereigns.

*Nyayadhish* - Chief Justice, dispensing justice on civil and criminal matters.

*Panditrao* - High Priest, managing internal religious matters.

Continued conflict with the Mughal Empire meant that military matters remained exceedingly important to the affairs of the nascent state. Hence, with the notable exception of the priestly *Panditrao* and the judicial *Nyayadisha*, the other *pradhans* held full-time military commands, and their deputies performed their civil duties in their stead. In the later era of the Maratha Empire, these deputies and their staff constituted the core of the Peshwa's bureaucracy.

## After Shivaji

Shivaji's son Sambhaji, (ruled 1680–89) undermined the importance of the council. Over time, council positions became hereditary, ceremonial positions at court with nominal powers, if any. Beginning 1714 AD, a prime minister appointed by Shivaji's grandson Shahu gradually arrogated power. Within a short period, *de facto* control of the Maratha state passed to his family. This family of hereditary prime ministers retained the title of *Peshwa.* However, the *Ashta Pradhan* council was never revived to fill the functions it discharged for the last decade of Shivaji's reign.

Miscellany:

- The Ashta Pradhan is somewhat similar to the court arrangements of other famous emperors such as the Navaratnas of the courts of both Vikramaditya and Akbar, as also of the Astadiggajas of Krishna Deva Raya's court.

- Lakshman Sen the ruler of the Sena Empire had *Pancharatnas* (meaning 5 gems) in his court; one of whom is believed to be Jayadeva, the famous Sanskrit poet and author of Gita Govinda.

- The Ashta Pradhan can be construed as an initiative to develop a second line of leadership in the state akin to the Khalsa by Guru Gobind Singh. Guru Gobind Singh and Shivaji were fighting against the Mughal emperor Aurangzeb.

❑❑❑

# Chapter 18

# His Legacy

He established a competent and progressive civil rule with the help of well-regulated and disciplined military and well-structured administrative organizations. He also innovated rules of military engagement, pioneering the "Shiva sutra" or *ganimi kava* (guerrilla tactics), which leveraged strategic factors like geography, speed, surprise and focused pinpoint attacks to defeat his larger and more powerful enemies. From a small contingent of 2,000 soldiers inherited from his father, he created a formidable force of 100,000 soldiers. He built and restored forts located strategically on land & sea for secure lands and coastline. He revived ancient Hindu political tradition & court conventions, and promoted Marathi and Sanskrit in court and administration usage. He is well known for his strong religious and warrior code of ethics and exemplary character. He was recognized as a great national hero during Indian Independence movement.

## Administration

The organization of Shivaji's administration was composed of eight ministers or *pradhaanas*:

· *Peshwa* - *Mukhya* (main) *Pradhan*, next to the king, for supervising and governing under king's orders in his absence. The king's orders bore the Peshwa's seal.

· *Mazumdar* - An auditor to take care of income and expenditure checks, keep the king informed of finances and sign districts-level accounts.

· *Navis* or *Waqia Mantri* - to record daily activities of the royal family and to serve as master of ceremony.

· *Sur Navis* or *Sachiv* - to oversee the king's correspondence to ensure letter and style adherence to wishes of the king and check accounts of palace and Parganas.

· *Sumant* or *Dabir* - for foreign affairs and to receive ambassadors.

· *Senapati* or *Sir-nobut* - To keep troops ready and the king fully informed.

· *Panditrao* - to promote learning, spirituality and settle religious disputes.

· Nyayadhish - the highest judicial authority.

**Military**

*Fig.: Statue of Chhatrapati Shivaji*

Shivaji demonstrated great skill in creating his military organisation, which lasted till the demise of the Maratha Empire. He was one of the pioneers of commando actions, then known as *ganimi kava*. His Mavala army's war cry was *Har Har Mahadev* ("Hail Lord Our God", *Har* and *Mahadev* being common names of Shiva). Shivaji was responsible for many significant changes in military organization:

- A standing army belonging to the state, called *paga*.
- All war horses belonged to the state; responsibility for their upkeep rested on the Sovereign.
- Creation of part time soldiers from peasants who worked for eight months in their fields and supported four months in war for which they were paid.
- Highly mobile and light infantry and cavalry excelling in commando tactics.
- The introduction of a centralized intelligence department; Bahirjee Naik was the foremost spy who provided Shivaji with enemy information in all of Shivaji's campaigns.
- A potent and effective navy.
- Introduction of field craft, such as guerrilla warfare, commando actions, and swift flanking attacks.
- Innovation of weapons and firepower, innovative use of traditional weapons like the tiger claw (*vaghnakh*) and *vita*.
- Militarisation of large swathes of society, across all classes, with the entire peasant population of settlements and villages near forts actively involved in their defence.

Shivaji realized the importance of having a secure coastline and protecting the western Konkan coastline from the attacks of Siddi's fleet. His strategy was to build a strong navy to protect and bolster his kingdom. He was also concerned about the growing dominance of British Indian naval forces in regional waters and actively sought to resist it. For this reason he is also referred to as the "Father of Indian Navy".

**Forts**

Shivaji captured strategically important forts at Murumbdev (Rajgad), Torana, Kondana (Sinhagad) and Purandar and laid the foundation of *swaraj* or self rule. Toward the end of his career, he had a control of 360 forts to secure his growing kingdom. Shivaji himself constructed about 15-20 totally new forts (including key sea forts like Sindhudurg), but he also rebuilt or repaired many strategically placed forts to create a chain of 300 or more, stretched over a thousand kilometres across the rugged crest of the Western Ghats. Each were placed under three officers of equal status lest a single traitor be bribed or tempted to deliver it to the enemy. The officers (sabnis, havladar, sarnobhat) acted jointly and provided mutual checks and balance.

**Navy**

Shivaji built a strong naval presence across long coast of Konkan and Goa to protect sea trade, to protect the lands from sack of prosperity of subjects from coastal raids, plunder and destruction by Arabs, Portuguese, British, Abyssinians and pirates. Shivaji started navy in Kalyan. Shivaji built ships in towns such as Kalyan, Bhivandi, and Goa for building fighting navy as well as trade. He also built a number of sea forts and bases for repair, storage and shelter. Shivaji fought many lengthy battles with Siddis of Janjira on coastline. The fleet grew to reportedly 160 to 700 merchant, support and fighting vessels. He started trading with foreigners on his own after possession of 8 or 9 ports in the Deccan.

## Promotion of Sanskrit

The house of Shivaji was well acquainted with Sanskrit and promoted the language; his father Shahaji had supported scholars such as Jayram Pindye, who prepared Shivaji's seal. Shivaji continued this Sanskrit promotion, giving his forts names such as Sindhudurg, Prachandgarh, and Suvarndurg. He named the *Ashta Pradhan* (council of ministers) as per Sanskrit nomenclature with terms such as Nyayadhish, and Senapat, and commissioned the political treatise *Rajya Vyavahar Kosh*. His Rajpurohit, Keshav Pandit, was himself a Sanskrit scholar and poet.

A significant aspect of Shivaji's rule was his attempt to revive ancient Hindu political tradition and court conventions. He introduced Marathi in the place of Persian as the court language, revived Sanskrit administrative nomenclature and compiled a dictionary of official terms, 'The Rajyavyavahar Kosh', to facilitate change over.

## Religious Policy: Secular Maratha Empire

Shivaji was a devout Hindu. He respected all religions within the region. Shivaji had great respect for other contemporary saints, most notably Samarth Ramdas for whom he had a lot of faith. Shivaji requested Ramdas swami to move his residence to a fort named Parali & establish his permanent monastery there. The fort was subsequently renamed "Sajjangad" - the fort of the sacred.Shivaji's son Sambhaji later on built a Samadhi temple of Samarth Ramdas swami on Sajjangad when Ramdas Swami left this world. The temple is very huge and totally built in Besalt stones in just 1.75 months. Samarth Ramdaas Swami also wrote a letter to Sambhaji Raje guiding him on what to do and what not to do after death of Shivaji Maharaj. This is a phenomenal historic letter and proof that describes how Shivaji Maharaj was.

Shivaji allowed his subjects freedom of religion and opposed forced conversion. The first thing Shivaji did after a conquest was to promulgate protection of mosques and Muslim tombs.

He commanded the respect and fealty of the Muslims under his command by his fair treatment of his friends as well as enemies. Kafi Khan, the Mughal historian and Francois Bernier, a French traveler, spoke highly of his religious policy. He also brought converts like Netaji Palkar and Bajaji back into Hinduism. Shivaji's sentiments of inclusivity and tolerance of other religions can be seen in an admonishing letter to Aurangzeb, in which he wrote:

Verily, Islam and Hinduism are terms of contrast. They are used by the true Divine Painter for blending the colours and filling in the outlines. If it is a mosque, the call to prayer is chanted in remembrance of Him. If it is a temple, the bells are rung in yearning for Him alone.

He had many Muslims in his military and ministries. His most trusted general in all his campaigns was Haider Ali Kohari; Darya Sarang was chief of armoury; Ibrahim Khan and Daulat Khan were prominent in the navy; and Siddi Ibrahim was chief of artillery. Shivaji had particular respect for the Sufi tradition of Islam. Shivaji used to pray at the mausoleum of the great Sufi Muslim saint Baba Sharifuddin. He also visited the abode of another great

Sufi saint, Shaikh Yacub of the Konkan, and took his blessings. He called Hazrat Baba of Ratnagiri - "bahut thorwale bhau", meaning "great elder brother". Thus, policy of inclusiveness of all sections of society in running the state also known as Maharashtra Dharma was founded by Shivaji.

Shivaji also promulgated other enlightened values, prohibiting slavery in his kingdom, and applying a humane and liberal policy to the women of his state.

## Character

Shivaji is noted for his strong religious and warrior code of ethics and exemplary character displayed during his long military career. He offered protection to houses of worship, non-combatants, women and children. He always showed respect, defended and protected places of worship of all denominations and religions.

Shivaji was once offered as a war booty an extremely beautiful young lady, by an uninformed Maratha captain. She was the daughter-in-law of a defeated Muslim Amir (local ruler) of Kalyan, Maharashtra. Shivaji was reported to have told the lady that her beauty was mesmerizing and He told her to go back to her family in peace, unmolested and under his protection. His behaviour, was noted by those around him, to be always of the highest moral caliber. He clearly and unambiguously embodied the virtues and ideals of a true nobleman.

He boldly risked his life, his treasure and his personal well being and that of his family, to openly challenge his immensely larger enemies to defend and achieve freedom and independence for his country. He did not spend any resources on projects designed for self-aggrandizement or vanity, instead he was propelled by his sense of dharma (sacred duty) to his people. The later Indian nationalists have hailed him as a role model for his heroism, selflessness, freedom, and courage. Shivaji earned a high level of admiration and respect from his followers and subjects. Even today, he is venerated in India and especially in the state of Maharashtra with awe and admiration and is viewed as a hero of epic proportions.

Swami Vivekanada considered Shivaji a hero and paid glowing tributes to his wisdom. When Lokmanya Tilak organized a festival to mark the birthday celebrations of Shivaji, Vivekananda agreed to preside over the festival in Bengal in 1901.

Shivaji died in April 1680, and his eldest son Sambhaji took power after being challenged by his stepmother Soyarabai. After the death of Shivaji, his widow Soyarabai Shirke started making plans with various ministers of the administration to replace Sambhaji with her son Raja Ram as the heir to the kingdom. On 21 April 1680, the ten-year old Raja Ram was installed in the throne. The news reached Sambhaji who was imprisoned in Panhala. On 27 April, he took possession of the fort after killing the commander and on 18 June, he acquired control of Raigarh. Sambhaji formally ascended the throne on 20 July, putting Soyarabai and Raja Ram in prison.

## Contemporary Foreign Accounts

Many foreign travellers who visited India during Shivaji Maharaj's time wrote about him. Abbe Carre was a French traveller who visited India around 1670; his account was published as *Voyage des Indes Orientales mêlé de plusieurs histories curieuses* at Paris in 1699. Some quotes:

Hardly had he won a battle or taken to town in one end of the kingdom than he was at the other extremity causing havoc everywhere and surprising important places. To this quickness of movement he added, like Julius Caesar, a clemency and bounty that won him the hearts of those his arms had worsted." "In his courage and rapidity he does not ill resemble the king of Sweden, Gustavus Adolphus.

The French traveller Francois Bernier wrote in his *Travels in Mughal India*:

*I forgot to mention that during pillage of Sourate, Seva-ji, the Holy Seva-ji! Respected the habitation of the reverend father Ambrose, the Capuchin missionary. 'The Frankish Padres are good men', he said 'and shall not be attacked.' He spared also the house of a deceased Delale or Gentile broker, of the Dutch, because assured that he had been very charitable while alive.*

Warriors and statesmen in India, Sir E.Sullivan:

*Shivaji possessed every quality requisite for success in the disturbed age in which he lived: cautious and wily in council, he was fierce and daring in action; he possessed an endurance that made him remarkable even amongst his hardy subjects, and an energy and decision that would in any age raised him to distinction.*

Cosme da Guarda says in "Life of the Celebrated Shivaji":

*Such was the good treatment Shivaji accorded to people and such was the honesty with which he observed the capitulations that none looked upon him without a feeling of love and confidence. By his people he was exceedingly loved. Both in matters of reward and punishment he was so impartial that while he lived he made no exception for any person; no merit was left unrewarded, no offence went unpunished; and this he did with so much care and attention that he specially*

*charged his governors to inform him in writing of the
conduct of his soldiers, mentioning in particular those
who had distinguished themselves, and he would at
once order their promotion, either in rank or in pay,
according to their merit. He was naturally loved by all
men of valor and good conduct.*

## The Creeper of Bharatiya Rajdharma

When describing Shivaji Maharaj his admirer Mr. M.S.
Vabgaonkar writes, "Shivaji is a radiant flower which has
blossomed from the Bharatiya creeper of Rajdharma. The
great promoter of Bharatiya Rajdharma, Kautilya in His
holy text the Arthashastra, has imagined an ideal king
and two thousand years later this king has taken birth in
the form of Shivaji. The king described by Kautilya was
one who emphasised on spying, who took full
responsibility for procuring all the benefits of an attack
onto himself, who was disinterested in worldly and sexual
pleasures and was well versed in law and religion besides
having an unblemished character and punishing subjects
only when required. Even this has proved right as per
Kautilya's description in case of Shivaji.

After 1920 the creeper of Bharatiya Rajdharma was
nurtured with the harmful manure of 'equality of all
religions', pleasing Muslims, etc. and thus from it sprang
a number of poisonous flowers in the form of Mohandas-
Jawaharlal or Manmohan-Soniya. To stop the blossoming
of such vicious flowers, the Bharatiya Rajdharma creeper
must be punished with the support of the Sanatan Vedic
religion and then watered with pure water from the Ganga
in the form of the biography of Shivaji Maharaj! When
this happens, then from every leaf of the creeper will
spring beautiful flowers like Chatrapati Shivaji Maharaj.
Only then will this creeper reach the skies.

□□□

# References

RaGajita Desâî; V. D. Katamble (2003). *Shivaji the Great*. Balwant Printers Pvt. Ltd.. p. 193. ISBN 81-902000-0-3.

"Finally, single Shiv Jayanti". *The Times of India* (Pune). 4 February 2003. Retrieved 27 January 2010.

Sen, Siba Pada (1973). *Historians and historiography in modern India*. Institute of Historical Studies. p. 106. Retrieved 6 March 2012.

Sarkar, Jadunath (1992). *Shivaji and his times* (5 ed.). Orient Longman. ISBN 81-250-1347-4.

N. Jayapalan (2001). *History of India*. Atlantic Publishers & Distri. p. 211. ISBN 978-81-7156-928-1.

Shivaji (Raja); S. L. Sharma (1974). *300th anniversary of coronation of Chatrapati Shivaji Maharaj: souvenir*. Foreign Window Pub.. Retrieved 2 October 2012.

Richard M. Eaton (17 November 2005) (in British English). *A Social History of the Deccan, 1300-1761: Eight Indian Lives*. 1. Location: Cambridge University Press. pp. 128–221. ISBN 978-0-521-25484-7. Retrieved 2 August 2012.

Stephen Meredyth Edwardes; Herbert Leonard Offley Garrett (1930). *Mughal Rule In India*. Atlantic Publishers & Dist. pp. 128–. ISBN 978-81-7156-551-1. Retrieved 2 October 2012.

http://books.google.com/books?id=04ellRQx4nMC&pg= PA441&lpg=PA441&dq=shivaji+pune+seal&source=bl&ots= 0ign2J3R3g&sig=wqwiGiTdsiCjkk01hwyW2gJL1I&hl= en&sa= X&ei=lcNtUO7wB6Tz0gHPz4CIDA&ved=0CEc Q6AEwBQ#v=onepage&q=shivaji%20pune%20seal&f=false

http://books.google.com/books?ei=wMJtUNqtLYb50g GPooCQCQ&id=c7ogAAAAMAAJ&dq=shivaji+yesaji+ maval&q=tanaji#search_anchorPg 105

Stewart Gordon (16 September 1993). *The Marathas 1600-1818.* Cambridge University Press. ISBN 978-0-521-26883-7. Retrieved 13 October 2012.

Caturbhuja (1987). *The Great Historical Dramas.* Mittal Publications. pp. 11–. GGKEY:UAKYDL2S8LK. Retrieved 28 September 2012.

Pearson, M.N. (February 1976). "Shivaji and the Decline of the Mughal Empire".*The Journal of Asian Studies* (Association for Asian Studies) 35 (2): 221–235. Retrieved 1 March 2012.

Vartak, Malavika (May 1999). "Shivaji Maharaj: Growth of a Symbol".*Economic and Political Weekly* (Economic and Political Weekly) 34 (19): 1126–1134. Retrieved 1 March 2012.

Jackson, William Joseph (2005). *Vijayanagara voices: exploring South Indian history and Hindu literature.* Ashgate Publishing, Ltd.. p. 38. ISBN 0-7546-3950-9, 9780754639503.

*The Cambridge History of India.*

Loch, W. *Dakhan History Musalman And Maratha, A.D. 1300 To 1818.* p. 592.

R. M. Betham (1908). *Maráthas and Dekhani Musalmáns.* Asian Educational Services. pp. 134–. ISBN 978-81-206-1204-4. Retrieved 27 September 2012.

Farooqui Salma Ahmed; Salma Ahmed Farooqui. *A Comprehensive History of Medieval India: From Twelfth to the Mid-Eighteenth Century.* Pearson Education India. pp. 317–. ISBN 978-81-317-3202-1. Retrieved 27 September 2012.

J. Nazareth (2008). *Creative Thinking in Warfare* (illustrated ed.). Lancer. pp. 174–176. ISBN 978-81-7062-035-8.

Nazareth, J. *Creative Thinking in Warfare.* p. 175.

Setumadhava Rao Pagdi (1983). *Shivaji.* National Book Trust, India. p. 29.

Vidya Dhar Mahajan (1967). *India since 1526.* S. Chand. p. 174.

Bentham, R M. *Maráthas and Dekhani Musalmáns.* p. 135.

Sharma, S.R. (1999). *Mughal empire in India: a systematic study including source material, Volume 2.* Atlantic Publishers & Dist. p. 59.

Mumford, David (1993). *The Marathas 1600-1818, Part 2, Volume 4.* Cambridge University Press. p. 71.

Ranade, Mahadeo Govind (2006 (1900 reprint)). *Rise of the Maratha Power.* Read Books. p. 35. ISBN 978-1-4067-3642-7. Retrieved 22 September 2008.

Pradeep Barua (1 May 2005). *The state at war in South Asia.* University of Nebraska Press. p. 42. ISBN 978-0-8032-1344-9. Retrieved 6 March 2012.

Mallavarapu Venkata Siva Prasada Rau; Andhra Pradesh Archives (1980). *Archival organization and records management in the state of Andhra Pradesh, India.* Published under the authority of the Govt. of Andhra Pradesh by the Director of State Archives (Andhra Pradesh State Archives). p. 393. Retrieved 30 September 2012.

Govind Sakharam Sardesai (1957). *New History of the Marathas: Shivaji and his line (1600-1707).* Phoenix Publications. p. 222. Retrieved 30 September 2012.

*Muslim India.* Muslim India. 2004. p. 1250. Retrieved 30 September 2012.

S. N. Sadasivan (October 2000). *A social history of India.* APH Publishing. p. 247.ISBN 978-81-7648-170-0. Retrieved 6 March 2012.

M. R. Kantak (1993). *The First Anglo-Maratha War, 1774-1783: A Military Study of Major Battles.* Popular Prakashan. pp. 18–. ISBN 978-81-7154-696-1. Retrieved 30 September 2012.

J. L. Mehta (1 January 2005). *Advanced Study in the History of Modern India: Volume One: 1707 - 1813.* Sterling Publishers Pvt. Ltd. pp. 707–. ISBN 978-1-932705-54-6. Retrieved 30 September 2012. - *It explains the rise to power of his Peshwa (prime minister) Buluji Vishwanath (171 3-20) and the transformation of the Maratha kingdom into a vast empire, by the collective action of all the Maratha stalwarts.*

Gijs Kruijtzer (20 June 2009). *Xenophobia in Seventeenth-Century India.* Amsterdam University Press. pp. 153–190. ISBN 978-90-8728-068-0. Retrieved 30 September 2012.

Krishnâjî Ananta Sabhâsada (1920). *Œiva Chhatrapati.* University of Calcutta. pp. 235–. Retrieved 30 September 2012. - *Therefore you will not have to serve the Bijapur Government personally, but in lieu of personal service you will have to send an army whenever ... These I have conferred on Ghimujlv Saubhagyavatl Dipa Bai for cholibangdl (pin money).*

Govind Sakharam Sardesai (1957). *New History of the Marathas: Shivaji and his line (1600-1707).* Phoenix Publications. p. 251. Retrieved 30 September 2012.

Maya Jayapal (1997). *Bangalore: the story of a city.* Eastwest Books (Madras). p. 20. ISBN 978-81-86852-09-5. Retrieved 30 September 2012. - *Shivaji's and Ekoji's armies met in battle on November 26, 1677, and Ekoji was defeated. By the treaty he signed, Bangalore and the adjoining areas were given to Shivaji, who then made them over to Ekoji's wife Deepabai to be held by her, with the proviso that Ekoji had to ensure that Shahji's samadhi was well tended.*

J. L. Mehta (1 January 2005). *Advanced Study in the History of Modern India: Volume One: 1707 - 1813.* Sterling Publishers Pvt. Ltd. p. 48. ISBN 978-1-932705-54-6. Retrieved 27 September 2012.

"History-Adilshahis, 1489-1686.". Gazetteer of the Bombay Presidency. Retrieved 27 February 2012.

Sunita Sharma; K2h2udâ Bak2h2sh Oriyanmal Pablik Lâ¼ibrerî (2004). *Veil, sceptre, and quill: profiles of eminent women, 16th-18th centuries.* Khuda Bakhsh Oriental Public Library. p. 139. Retrieved 30 September 2012. - *By June, 1680 three months after Shivaji's death Rajaram was made a prisoner in the fort of Raigad, along with his mother Soyra Bai and his wife Janki Bai. Soyra Bai was put to death on charge of conspiracy*

*Gazetteer of the Bombay Presidency: Sátára.* Government Central Press. 1885. pp. 249–. Retrieved 30 September 2012.

Ramesh Chandra Majumdar (1974). *The Mughul Empire.* B.V. Bhavan. pp. 609, 634. Retrieved 27 September 2012.

Abraham Eraly (2000). *Emperors of the Peacock Throne: The Saga of the Great Mughals.* Penguin Books India. ISBN 978-0-14-100143-2. Retrieved 27 September 2012.

Kincaid, Charles; Parasnis, Dattaray (1918). *A History of the Maratha People.* 1. London: Oxford University Press. pp. 183–194

Rafiq Zakaria (2002). *Communal Rage In Secular India.* Popular Prakashan.ISBN 978-81-7991-070-2. Retrieved 26 September 2012.

American Oriental Society (1963). *Journal of the American Oriental Society.* American Oriental Society.. p. 476. Retrieved 27 September 2012.

"Indian Naval Hospital Ship INHS Dhanvantari". Indiannavy.nic.in. 25 August 2010. Retrieved 27 September 2010.

Kasar, D.B. (2005). Rigveda to Raigarh making of Shivaji the great. Manudevi Prakashan.

http://books.google.com/books?id=qweZWra_tbwC&pg=PA28&lpg=PA28&dq=ganimi+kava&source=bl&ots=JkK0OXr_4&sig=esV1pDNiyrjQvfSDw2vgQQ3aEWU&hl=en&sa=X&ei=ssNrUPrhCs-v0AGRkYH4Dw&ved=0CEkQ6AEwBQ#v=onepage&q=ganimi%20kava&f=false

Setumadhavarao S. Pagadi., Setumadhavarao S (1993) (in Pagadi). *Shivaji.* National Book Trust. p. 21. ISBN 81-237-0647-2.

Pagdi, Setumadhava Rao (1983). *Shivaji.* India: National Book Trust, India.ISBN B0006CNKM2.

Indian Armed Forces, Bharat Verma, Lancer Publishers, 2008, ISBN 0-9796174-2-1, ISBN 978-0-9796174-2-3

http://books.google.co.in/books?id=V4-Su0whKa0C&pg=PA137&redir_esc=y#v=onepage&q&f=false

http://books.google.co.in/books?id=V4-Su0whKa0C&pg=PA137&redir_esc=y#v=onepage&q&f=false

G. S Banhatti (1995). *Life And Philosophy Of Swami Vivekananda.* Atlantic Publishers & Dist. p. 201. ISBN 978-81-7156-291-6.

Jayasree Mukherjee (1997). *The Ramakrishna-Vivekananda movement impact on Indian society and politics (1893-1922): with special reference to Bengal.* Firma KLM.ISBN 978-81-7102-057-7.

"comments : Modi unveils Shivaji statue at Limbayat". Indianexpress.com. Retrieved 2012-09-17.

Karline McLain (11 February 2009). *India's Immortal Comic Books: Gods, Kings, and Other Heroes.* Indiana University Press. pp. 137–. ISBN 978-0-253-22052-3. Retrieved 26 September 2012.

PTI (2009-09-15). "News / National : President inaugurates Shivaji memorial building in Delhi". The Hindu. Retrieved 2012-09-17.

Pune Mirror (2012-05-16). "New Shivaji statue faces protests". Punemirror.in. Retrieved 2012-09-17.

"Kalam unveils Shivaji statue". The Hindu. 2003-04-29. Retrieved 2012-09-17.

"INS Shivaji (Engineering Training Establishment): Training". Indian Navy. Retrieved 2012-09-17.

"Chhatrapati Shivaji Maharaj". Indianpost.com. 1980-04-21. Retrieved 2012-09-17.

The author has posted comments on this article (2012-06-17). "Bank notes: RBI considers other noteworthy icons - The Times of India". Timesofindia.indiatimes.com. Retrieved 2012-09-17.

Sir Edward Robert Sullivan (1866). *The conquerors, warriors, and statesmen of India: an historical narrative of the principal events from the invasion Mahmoud of Ghizni to that of Nader Shah.* John Murray. pp. 384–. Retrieved 26 September 2012.

Bharatiya Vidya Bhavan; Bhâratîya Itihâsa Samiti (1951). *The History and Culture of the Indian People: The Maratha supremacy.* G. Allen & Unwin. Retrieved 26 September 2012.

□□□

# Index

## A

Adilshahi Forces, 46, 47, 50, 54, 73, 74, 138, 143, 146, 150, 152, 155, 156, 157, 159, 166.

Administration, 6, 12, 13, 17, 26, 33, 35, 36, 65, 100, 105, 121, 122, 176, 205, 217, 218, 219, 221, 228.

Aftermath, 142, 152, 172, 192, 211.

Afzal Khan, 1, 44, 45, 46, 73, 74, 88, 89, 91, 96, 116, 118, 136, 137, 138, 139, 140, 141, 142, 143, 144, 145, 146, 148, 149, 151, 155, 169, 174, 198.

Arthashastra, 230.

Ashta Pradhan, 217, 219, 220, 225.

## B

Baji Rao I, 8, 18, 19.

Balaji Baji Rao, 20.

Balaji Vishwanath, 15, 39.

Battle, 7, 8, 12, 13, 19, 23, 25, 27, 37, 43, 46, 47, 52, 53, 57, 59, 60, 62, 63, 69, 70, 81, 82, 91, 103, 119, 123, 139, 143, 150, 155, 156, 157, 159, 163, 164, 165, 166, 167, 169, 170, 171, 172, 176, 181, 185, 186, 187, 188, 190, 191, 192, 195, 196, 208, 228.

Battle of Chakan, 173.

Battle of Kolhapur, 47, 155.

Battle of Nesari, 60.

Battle of Pavan Khind, 51, 52, 146, 159, 162.

Battle of Pratapgad, 44, 136, 141, 143, 146.

Battle of Purander, 43.

Battle of Salher, 59.

Battle of Sinhgad, 59.

Battle of Umberkhind, 53, 169.

Battle of Vani-dindori, 59.

Bharatiya Rajdharma, 230.

British Intervention, 27.

## C

Campaigns, 36, 59, 76, 93, 217, 223, 226.

Changing Alliances, 131.

Chhatrapati Rajaram, 12, 13, 17, 38, 39.

Chhatrapati Sambhaji, 11, 38, 39, 162.

Chhatrapati Shahu, 14, 38, 39.

Chhatrapati Shivaji, 3, 9, 11, 38, 92, 94, 107, 108, 109, 111, 112, 119, 144, 155, 161, 164, 169, 181, 208, 213, 217, 222.

Chimnajee Madhavarao, 40.

## E

Empire, 223, 225.

## F

Forts, 1, 12, 13, 17, 43, 52, 53, 57, 59, 63, 65, 80, 85, 99, 104, 105, 109, 116, 117, 118, 121, 122, 124, 130, 132, 134, 135, 136, 138, 144, 150, 151, 153, 154, 155, 159, 167, 185, 186, 188, 192, 194, 200, 206, 210, 214, 215, 216, 218, 221, 223, 224, 225.

## G

Ganimi Kava, 4, 221, 223.

## H

Hirdas Maval, 85.

Holkar, 8, 9, 16, 23, 26, 27, 28, 29, 30, 31, 32, 40.

## I

Inayat Khan, 43, 181, 182.

## J

Jijabai, 40, 41, 42, 62, 67, 69, 71, 73, 74, 75, 76, 77, 83, 84, 85, 141, 149.

Jinji, 2, 13, 17, 63, 194, 200, 201, 202, 203, 204, 205, 206.

## L

Lal Mahal, 55, 79, 82, 83, 84, 178.

## M

Madhavrao Peshwa, 7, 8, 25, 39.

Maharaja Yashwantrao Holkar, 30.

Maharani Tarabai, 12, 38.

Maharashtra, 19, 25, 40, 64, 67, 68, 69, 70, 78, 85, 87, 91, 92, 93, 96, 107, 108, 124, 126, 141, 143, 148, 151, 152, 155, 159, 160, 169, 181, 183, 185, 188, 194, 200, 208, 210, 217, 227, 228.

Maratha, 3, 4, 5, 7, 8, 9, 10, 12, 13, 14, 15, 16, 17,

19, 20, 21, 23, 25, 26, 27, 28, 29, 31, 32, 33, 34, 35, 36, 37, 38, 45, 46, 47, 49, 51, 53, 54, 55, 56, 57, 59, 60, 61, 63, 64, 65, 66, 67, 69, 71, 82, 87, 88, 89, 91, 94, 96, 99, 100, 104, 105, 121, 123, 124, 126, 127, 128, 130, 132, 135, 138, 139, 140, 143, 145, 146, 147, 150, 151, 153, 154, 155, 156, 157, 159, 161, 162, 164, 165, 167, 169, 172, 173, 174, 177, 178, 179, 181, 182, 184, 185, 187, 188, 190, 193, 194, 195, 196, 197, 198, 199, 200, 201, 203, 204, 205, 206, 207, 208, 209, 210, 211, 213, 214, 216, 217, 218, 220, 223, 225, 227.

Maratha Empire, 3, 4, 7, 8, 9, 10, 12, 13, 16, 17, 19, 25, 28, 29, 34, 35, 36, 37, 46, 65, 67, 69, 99, 104, 143, 146, 147, 151, 154, 159, 162, 173, 184, 193, 194, 207, 208, 210, 218, 220, 223, 225.

Maratha Forces, 20, 23, 49, 54, 60, 61, 64, 173, 182, 184, 199, 216.

Moreshwar Pingale, 39.

Mughal, 3, 7, 8, 10, 12, 13, 14, 15, 23, 25, 26, 27, 31, 36, 38, 43, 46, 47, 48, 49, 53, 54, 55, 56, 57, 58, 64, 69, 70, 71, 73, 75, 78, 84, 87, 89, 90, 91, 94, 100, 101, 102, 105, 108, 109, 111, 118, 121, 122, 123, 124, 126, 127, 128, 129, 131, 133, 134, 135, 136, 141, 142, 152, 161, 169, 173, 174, 175, 176, 177, 178, 179, 181, 182, 183, 184, 185, 187, 192, 193, 194, 195, 196, 198, 199, 200, 201, 202, 203, 204, 205, 206, 207, 208, 209, 210, 211, 213, 214, 217, 219, 220, 226, 229.

# N

Nana Sahib, 40.

Narayanrao Bajirao, 39.

# P

Parshuram Tribak Kulkarni, 39.

Peninsular India, 126.

Peshwa Bajirao, 16, 39.

Peshwa Era, 16.

Political Geography, 126.

Purandar, 1, 56, 57, 122, 185, 186, 187, 188, 192, 213, 214, 215, 224.

# Q

Queen Tarabai, 38, 39.

## R

Ramchandra Pant Amatya Bawdekar, 13, 17.

Royal Era, 9.

## S

Secular Maratha Empire, 225.

Shaiste Khan, 84.

Shivaji Maharaj, 226, 230.

Shyampant Kulkarni-Ranzekar, 39.

Siege of Panhala, 48, 50, 169.

Soldier, 32, 33, 69, 208.

Sonopant Dabir, 39.

Succession Crisis, 63.

Sultanate, 3, 4, 10, 42, 43, 70, 75, 100, 124, 129, 137, 194, 205.

## W

War, 4, 8, 13, 15, 17, 19, 20, 27, 29, 30, 31, 32, 38, 64, 72, 76, 78, 104, 124, 127, 128, 131, 134, 135, 153, 185, 193, 194, 201, 202, 203, 207, 209, 211, 213, 214, 223, 227.

□□□

www.ingramcontent.com/pod-product-compliance
Lightning Source LLC
Chambersburg PA
CBHW020809100426
42814CB00014B/385/J